CROWDSOURCING
PARIS

CROWDSOURCING PARIS

MEMOIRS OF A PARIS ADVENTURE

J.H. BUNTING

CROWDSOURCE ADVENTURE

∼

For Seth, the inciter of many incidents,
and for the readers of The Write Practice.

We shall remember ... the oldest metropolis on earth, the one city in all the world that has kept its name and held its place and looked serenely on while the Kingdoms and Empires of four thousand years have risen to life, enjoyed their little season of pride and pomp, and then vanished and been forgotten!

—Mark Twain

PROLOGUE

I was going to die there, I was sure, sixty feet below Paris in a tunnel named after a street I couldn't pronounce the name of, steps from the bones of six million dead, lost at the crossroads of three tunnels. I had no idea where I was or what I was going to do.

For the last several months, I had been in over my head in this city, metaphorically and now literally. For months, I had been barely scraping my way through a series of adventures. Some were exciting, some were uncomfortable, but all of them had led to better stories than I could ever have made back home.

But now, on the night before I was supposed to leave Paris, I was wondering if this was the end, not just of my adventures but of my life.

In my hand was the smallest flashlight in the world. Literally, the smallest in the world. It was a single bulb LED lamp that, when I bought it at the outdoor store in the Latin quarter, had the description "the smallest flashlight in the world" written on the package. The only reason I bought it was because I didn't have enough money for anything better. When I turned it on, I could see a grand total of five feet in front of me.

Even worse, I was standing next to a cave-in (yes, I was in a cave where a cave-in had occurred). I listened for the sound of the tunnel collapsing above me and heard only silence. It wasn't very comforting.

So that was it. There, in that tunnel sixty feet below the City of Light, I was doomed to spend the last few hours I had left on earth.

I pointed my flashlight down one tunnel. It was taller than most, twelve feet, maybe fourteen, and wide, wider than I was tall, with a gentle slope up. But I couldn't see the end of it with my pitiful light and I had no idea where it led.

I had hoped to find the beach. It was supposed to be a large room with sandy floors and a wave painted on one wall—thus the name. People went there for underground parties, and I imagined stumbling onto one and joining in on the adventure. There was a reproduction of the Mona Lisa there, too, and thousands of other graffiti pieces.

To my right was the cave-in. Before it collapsed, I wondered if the cataphiles had been digging a secret room. In 2004 the police found a gallery equipped with an under-ground movie theater, including a full-sized screen, a projector, reel-to-reel films, and a security system that played a recording of barking dogs if intruders got too close. The police came back a week later and it was gone, all except for a note that said, "Do not try to find us." Perhaps this was the beginning of a new theater. Was the cave-in beside me meant to be a similar place?

I looked back the way I came. The light didn't shine that far back and all I saw was a ring of darkness. Somewhere back there, though, were two parallel tunnels that led underneath the Luxembourg Gardens, where I had first entered. I had been going too fast, though. There were too many turns, too many tunnels half filled with water, too many crawl throughs. I could not visualize my way back.

I pointed the light down at my feet. The limestone dust caked my sneakers pale. *You won't really die down here*, I told myself. *You will find someone, a cataphile. They will help you.*

Yes, but who else would come down there tonight? It was past midnight. Cataphiles usually visit at night so they're not seen entering and exiting, but would they be out this late? Would one find me tomorrow? Or the next night? Two nights of dehydration and exposure in the caves, could I survive that?

Not far from here were the bones of six million of Paris' dead. I had seen a few of them already when I passed a brick wall different from the others and turned down a narrow passage to see the splintered bones scattered along the floor.

I thought of Philibert Aspairt, whose underground grave I had passed an hour ago. I thought of his death, alone and lost and confused. I thought of the girl melted into the floor in the tunnels below Odessa. It had taken them years to find her desiccated body huddled in a stain of her own blood and fluids. She had probably wandered around the caves disoriented for several days until dehydration stopped her and she huddled into a ball, going in and out of consciousness until she slowly died. Her name had been Masha. She was nineteen. There are 170 miles of tunnels underneath Paris, a lot of space to lose a body. I wondered how long it would take them to find mine.

You can find your way out of here if you know the

streets. Each tunnel was built underneath a corresponding street aboveground. They are all labeled. Before I stopped here to get my bearings, I passed a sign chiseled into the wall that said Rue de Frère, a street that no longer exists. These tunnels were labeled in the late 1700s and many of the streets have been gone for centuries. But if you keep walking, you can find tunnels that do still match the street names above. If you know the streets, you know the tunnels.

But I didn't know the streets of Paris, even after living here for months. I was lost without a map, without even the stars or sun to guide me.

Limestone is like a sponge. It soaks in water, light, and sound. You could scream in those tunnels and a hundred feet away, no one would hear you.

I turned off my flashlight. It was not a very good flashlight. I had only been able to see a few feet in front of me, but with it off the darkness was absolute. You cannot comprehend darkness like this when you are in light. It is darkness beyond understanding, without even a pinprick to orient your eyes. Darkness becomes a *thing*, as if the world has *become* darkness, as if the world itself ceases to exist. I wondered, would I cease to exist?

I was supposed to leave Paris tomorrow. A bus would take me and Talia to the airport an hour and a half outside of town. But Talia was asleep sixty feet up and miles away. She could not find me down here.

There had been other exits. I had passed ladders going up through the ceiling. One might lead to a manhole cover on the streets above. I could walk back and try to find one. I could climb the ladder. I would not look down. I would pray to not slip.

But it would be pointless. The entrances to these unsanctioned catacombs were all welded shut, and that meant the exits were welded shut as well, all but the one I had come from, not that I knew how to get back to it.

I was in a tomb. The bones of Paris' dead were with me. I looked out into the darkness but there was nothing to see.

My only thought, *I was going to die for a stupid book?*

1

PARIS

In the spirit of Benjamin Franklin, Mark Twain, Ernest Hemingway, and Tim Ferriss, travel the world and write about your experience. (From Joe B.)

∼

"It sounds, I don't know how to say it, kind of selfish and boring," Max had said.

It was a month before our flight. We were living in Talia's parents' basement, had moved out of our apartment to save money for France. But when I added up our budget, I realized that we would be $600 short of what we needed to live in Paris. How was I going to find $600 and keep this trip alive? My first thought had been to sell the guitar I had since I was sixteen, that I had traveled from California to Georgia with when I first started dating Talia. *Paris was worth it*, I thought.

"Aren't you a writer?" a friend told me. "Can't you come up with some other way to make $600 with your writing?"

"Huh," I thought, and that's where the idea to write a

book, a travelogue about living Paris with my wife and ten-month-old son came from.

Except Max hated the idea.

"Paris is kind of tame, you know?" he said. "I don't know if that alone will make a very good story."

I had been a fan of Max's writing before I ever met him. He was on a long road trip at the time, Jack Keroacking his way through America, staying in campgrounds and on people's couches, writing short stories in coffee shops in the midwest and blogging about the whole experience. To me, Max represented a kind of hipster coolness that didn't care about money and just wanted to make great art.

"What can you do to make it more adventurous?" he asked.

I hated Max so much in that moment.

All I wanted out of Paris was to sit in cafés, to soak in the atmosphere, to people watch to my heart's content, and describe all my surroundings and emotions while doing it, you know, how Hemingway did it.

Wasn't it enough to travel to Paris with not enough money and a ten-month-old? What more do you want from me?!

"Do what you want, man," said Max. "It's your book. But you asked me if I thought people would finance this book, and because you have a big audience, I think you can probably get $600. I just don't think it will be a very good book."

I felt like a fraud. Here I was *teaching* people to write books, and I was being told my book idea was terrible.

Not long after that I was walking around my in-law's farm, brainstorming on my book project, when I ran into Seth.

"I was thinking about your book," he said.

Uh oh, I thought. *Here comes an idea.*

My father-in-law Seth is an idea guy. He walks on his treadmill all day thinking up ideas and emailing them to people. He's written a couple of books and many of his ideas are brilliant . . . for someone, not necessarily for me.

"What your book needs is more adventure," he said. "You need to have a whole series of adventures."

"Adventures? What do you mean?"

"The problem is, Paris isn't adventurous enough. It has great food and great ambience, but ambience doesn't make a great story. Maybe you interview ten people on the street. Or, you know, there were those riots and car burnings a few years ago. You could go to that neighborhood and interview people about what happened."

It sounded horrible to me. All I *wanted* was ambience. I wanted cafés. I wanted to soak in the artistic atmosphere. I wanted cheap French wine and museums and bookstores. I wanted to live the writer's life in Paris.

I did NOT want to talk to random strangers every day! And I definitely did NOT want to interview Islamists in a slummy neighborhood forty minutes away from the city center.

I didn't tell Seth that, of course.

"Wow. Yeah . . . that's a really good idea," I said. "I kind of feel like just going to Paris with a baby will be adventure enough, though, don't you?"

He just grunted and went back to his pacing.

Even as Seth and Max oddly echoed each other, I didn't want to admit I knew they had a point. I began to feel my perfect trip to Paris slipping through my fingers. But before I caved into Seth's and Max's demands for adventure, I knew I had one more possible out: my audience.

If my audience didn't think it was a good idea, I wouldn't have to do it.

For the last few years, I had been writing online. I shared my writing process, the things I was learning about being a writer, and how other people could become writers too. When I first started, my goal had been to have a thousand subscribed readers, but to my surprise, by this point, I had over a hundred thousand people reading my writing every month.

So after I finished talking with Seth, I sent out an email to my audience, mentioning the book idea, praying that they would hate it. Then, I closed my laptop and started packing.

I WOKE up with a start to find a gaggle of teenage girls staring at me. To my shame, I was at a Starbucks a few blocks down Boulevard Saint Germain, and only because it had free wifi, unlike the other Parisian cafés I had tried to write at. I sat up, wiped the drool off my face, and checked my watch.

Shit, I had been out for thirty minutes. Or what do the French say? *Merde.* We had arrived in Paris just four days before, and I was already behind.

How did I get into this mess? I thought as I opened the list of adventures I had been given.

I could have been sitting at a streetside café, writing my book, glancing up to daydream about the city, eavesdropping on the conversations of my neighbors. Instead, I was stuck in the most clichéd chain in the world drinking the worst coffee I'd ever had and buried in the expectations of a hundred thousand people.

After Seth and Max had conspired to force feed my life more adventure, I had sent out an email to my audience explaining this new book idea.

"I'm thinking about writing a crowdsourced memoir,"

the email said. " Here's how it could work: you suggest an adventure. Then, I do what you say. For example, you suggest, 'Strike up a conversation in broken French with three people today.' I say, 'Oui.' You say, 'Take a picture in each of the twenty arrondissements in one day.' I say, "Why of course.'"

I hoped it wouldn't work. I hoped people would say, "That's a weird idea," and ignore it, archive the email and never think of it again. My biggest fear was that they would take it seriously.

And that fear was realized.

Of course it was.

Immediately after I posted it, adventures for my new book started coming in from people all over the world.

There was the dance they had chosen for me to do in front of the Arc de Triomphe, for example, my best rendition of "Singing in the Rain." Hint: even my best rendition is just about the worst dance you've ever seen in your life.

As if that bit of public humiliation wasn't enough, they had also ordered me to job shadow a street performer, then perform the routine I learned outside of Notre Dame. I really hated that one.

Some were strange, like this creepily specific challenge: "Meet a random stranger on the terrace of the Café Le Horse on Saturday, March fifteenth (they may or may not be wearing a hat and reading the newspaper)."

Others were literary, like this one: "Follow a storyline of Paris in the 1789 revolution: *Tale of Two Cities*, or *Les Miserables*. How do those events compare with the 1968 student strikes on the Left Bank and the 2013 car burnings by Muslim youth?" Actually, that didn't sound so bad.

And there were many that were touristy: "Take a picture of yourself while doing every cliché of visiting Paris. A few ideas: get a picture in front of all the famous landmarks: the Eiffel Tower, Notre Dame, the Louvre Pyramid, Shakespeare and Co. bookshop, etc." Some good ideas, but way too much ground to cover.

They even wanted control of my diet: eat tripe, the told me, the stomach lining of a cow. Excuse me as I vomit.

And of course, there was the pièce de résistance: to explore the 170-mile network of caves and catacombs beneath Paris. Please kill me. Better yet, one of those tunnels would be the perfect spot. You wouldn't even have to bury my body. I'd already be sixty feet under and surrounded by bones and skeletons. Perfect, right?

There were dozens more, some of which were plausible and some which were absolutely insane.

What I had wanted out of Paris was to walk through the city soaking in the beauty, to sit in the most inspiring cafés in the world, to write, to drink coffee and wine, and to feel like a real writer.

What I got was a dirty Starbucks, a disgusting cup of coffee, and a feeling like I was trying to fake this and failing. How was I going to make *this* into a good story? How was I going to to do this?

As I sorted through the adventures people suggested with a growing sense of dread, I knew it would make for a far better book. At the same time, I also knew that my least favorite game in the world is truth or dare.

I cursed Max. I cursed my father-in-law.

"Hey man. I think this trip is brilliant," one person told me. "I hope it's awesome for you."

"I am very happy to support your adventure in Paris with your wife and son," said another.

"I love having a front row seat!" said one more.

I hate all of you, I thought.

The worst part was when people started sending money to make their suggestions happen. Most gave twenty or thirty dollars, but one day I checked my email to find someone gave a thousand dollars. I hated that person the most. I could have ignored it before, but now I was beginning to feel financially obligated to follow through with this.

YOU MIGHT NOT BELIEVE I'm so anti-adventure. Perhaps an adventure, to you, is something you *live* for, are craving for. Perhaps that's why you're reading this book.

But the truth is my perfect moment is not a heart-pounding, risk-filled exploit, but a cup—or better, a carafe—of strong coffee in an outdoor café. Switch out a bottle of Vueve or a gin and tonic as the sun is going down, and it would have the makings of the perfect day.

And while I have had a few adventures—I've rafted the Nile in Uganda, pet tigers in Thailand, and skinny dipped on four continents; I've devoured pig steaks skewered on sticks cooked over a bonfire fire in Transylvania, eaten grilled dog in Cambodia, and sipped lentil soup every day during a cold month in Turkey—I would trade it all for a long day at one of my favorite cafés in Santa Barbara.

Once, in 2010, I had just flown to Thailand from Kenya. I found myself staying with a young Thai farming family in the jungle just beside the border to Myanmar. My days were spent cutting down banana trees to feed the cows and mixing concrete for a new barn. My nights were spent lying under a mosquito net watching bootlegged movies off a flash drive.

The only problem, besides the heat and the spider bites, was that it was my birthday. The jungles of Thailand are good for many things, but not for birthdays.

The only birthday gift I wanted was to go to the coffee shop—there was only one within fifty miles. Once there, I hoped to sit all day and write in my journal, or maybe just stare out the window at the big, vine-wrapped trees pressing in on the roads everywhere in that town. There was a stream and a small waterfall beside the road and I imagined taking breaks from my writing to walk beside it and stare into the water, then walk back and drink another Thai coffee sweetened with condensed milk until I was antsy and inspired.

So we got in the truck to go into town, and we began driving through the jungle. And we kept driving. And driving.

After the first hour, I started to get carsick. After the second hour, I started to feel like the trip was taking a little long. After the third hour, I started to realize, huh, maybe there's been some misunderstanding? Maybe they don't do birthdays in Thailand.

I thought about saying, "Um, weren't you supposed to stop at my coffee shop, oh, I don't know, four hours ago?"

But when you're a guest and you're in a truck with fifteen other fellow guest laborers and you're not really sure how well your host speaks English or if they even celebrate birthdays in Thailand, you don't ask a lot of questions.

Five hours later, I finally stumbled out of the car at a tourist-trap waterfall park.

"Your coffee shop," my host said, pointing to a collection of cheap, outdoor restaurants. And then he left and walked up to the waterfalls.

All I wanted was a real coffee shop with air conditioning, and instead I got more ninety-five degree, thousand percent humidity heat, and flies that buzzed into my ear every time I tried to write the letter "e." Even worse, the Thai coffee wasn't even that good.

I wrote in my journal for five minutes, mostly about how annoyed I was, sweating in the impossibly humid air, and then gave up and walked into the forest.

It was beautiful. The trees looked like redwoods. The wide path followed the lazy river rolling over big mossy rocks. It was somehow cool there, beneath the canopy, and dancing in the stream were those little fish that nibble at your toes and exfoliate your skin, fish that they have in neon lit streets all over Southeast Asia. Here, though, it felt authentic and encouraging to know you could find these same fish in an actual pond in a beautiful park where you could sit on a rock and let them nibble you. I looked at the giant trees and slow moving currents for what felt like hours. I took my notebook out and wrote a few lines that felt, at least as I was writing them, like poetry. I didn't want to leave.

This is both why I hate adventures and find myself frequently in their midst. Adventures make for good stories, but like Thai flies, they often distract from that deep soul work you can only do in solitude and stillness. Even as I've seen the most amazing natural wonders in my travels, I've always fantasized about pulling out a café table and breaking out an espresso pot, making up a quick macchiato, and only then sitting there, taking it all in. Can the lessons of nature truly be contemplated without a beverage? Where would I store all this equipment though? My camel? My sherpa? It's always the logistics that ruin the fun!

I'm a writer, though, and the American literary tradition requires adventure.

Benjamin Franklin, my nation's founding father—who lived in Paris for eight years, by the way—said, "Either write something worth reading or do something worth writing."

The great American writers have always taken that as a

challenge to do both. Ernest Hemingway shot lions on safari in East Africa, John Steinbeck took a ship around Cape Horn and worked as an itinerant laborer in Baja, Jack Kerouac hitch-hiked across America, and Byron had sex with a lot of men and a few women (no, he wasn't American, but he fit the tradition).

And I wanted to be a great writer. Needed to be one.

I once met an innkeeper in Rhonda, Spain who, as a little girl, had seen Hemingway sitting at a cafe drinking a glass of beer. He had been in town for the bullfights, which were very famous there. She was in her late sixties when I met her, and though I can't remember what she looked like, I can still remember the image I had in my mind as she told the story, of Hemingway in a white shirt unbuttoned to his chest, his grey hair slicked back, and his big arms holding a glass to his lips. It struck me that just seeing him was a memory she kept all her life.

Could I have that too? Could I create these memories, these markers in a life well lived? Could my work be part of how people defined themselves? Could my life hold up to my dreams for it?

I was so confident it could, then, and I thought Paris was a step to finding out.

I had so much to learn.

IT WOULD HAVE BEEN SO MUCH EASIER to return everyone's money and say, "Just kidding. Sorry for my stupid idea!" It would have been so much more comfortable to throw away the list of adventures people from all over the world sent in.

But I didn't do that. I said yes. We were going to Paris. And like it or not, it was going to be an adventure.

I placed my laptop back in my bag, slung it around my shoulder, and left.

Walking home from that Starbucks on Boulevard Saint German, I realized that while I truly had no idea what I was doing in Paris, while I felt out of my depth, lost in the darkness of my own adventure, I also knew the worse it got for me the better the story would be afterward.

If I had to live an adventure, I was going to do it right.

And as I looked at the beautiful Parisian buildings around me, I knew that somehow, and I really didn't know how at that moment, I had to get into the illegal catacombs under Paris.

The Twelve Adventures

1. In the spirit of Benjamin Franklin, Mark Twain, Ernest Hemingway, and Tim Ferriss, travel the world and write about your experience.
   (From me)
2. Explore the huge system of caverns, caves and catacombs underground below Paris, left from when the Romans quarried the whole place for stone, and every once in a while a bit of Paris plunges into a hole. (From Dan Knight)
3. Select a destination (any destination) in Paris and see if you can find your way there using only the locals for help. You must speak only French!
   (From Kate)
4. Père Lachaise Cimetière awaits you. Hunt down the gravesites of Molière, Richard Wright, Balzac, Proust and Colette, commune with their ghosts, and leave a flower at each. Over a million people

are buried there, some on thirty year leases. Sorry to say, you can no longer leave kisses in red lipstick on Oscar Wilde's monument, as it is encased in a protective covering; or spend the night at Jimmy Morrison's grave, as it is guarded now by bouncers. Even so, it's fun to watch others try! (From Julia W.)

5. Do your best rendition of "Singing in the Rain" in front of the Arc de Triomphe. (From Annie Carter)

6. Become a street performer at Notre Dame. First, you have to meet the current street performers and learn their trade. They are the main character and you are the sidekick learning from their expertise. Are they just homeless bums who beg? Or are they experts in their craft? Do they struggle to just get a few pennies or do they make serious bank off their entertainment? Why do they do it? At the same time, you overcome your "writer self" and put yourself out there to perform ... be watched, be criticized, be viewed by people who don't know who you really are and are just judging their perception of you. You become them. Ready ... Go! (From Laura J.)

7. Eat onion soup at Les Halles and find out why it has become an institution. (From Winnie)

8. Job shadow a chef. (From anonymous)

9. Visit an art supply shop, and buy some watercolors and quality paper. Paint your best painting. Then head over to the Pont des Arts and set up a crate or table and try to sell them! (From Margaret)

10. Eat tripe. (From anonymous)

11. Romance your wife in an unexpected way. I picture this looking like you bringing her along on your day of adventures (get a babysitter that she trusts perhaps) and plant someone near the end of the day who will tell you they really need your help, or they have to show you something and they will take you two to a beautifully-set table overlooking the romantic sights of Paris or something. (From Ross B.)

12. Visit ten museums in Paris. Write about what you see, as well as the comments you have exchanged when you were before each of the exhibitions in those museums. (From Paul N.)

Challenge no. 1: Travel

The best stories come from adventure. Comfort, security, routines—these are all great things, but they're also the enemies of story. Every adventure requires three things:

1. Journey. Adventure requires some kind of distance traveled. The journey can be as short as a walk to another room or as long as the distance to someone's heart.

2. Destination. Adventures always have a goal, some kind of end place. The destination might be a place, a prize, or an achievement, but without some kind of goal, there is no drama.

3. Risk. Adventures upset the status quo. Without the potential for pain, there can be no upside.[1]

My hope for this book is not just that you would get to hear about *my* uncomfortable adventures, but that you would be inspired to go on adventures of *your own*, whether they be in Paris or closer to home.

That's why throughout this book I will be challenging you to go on your *own* adventures. You could skip over them on your way to the next chapter. You could skim through them and say, "Hmm . . . that sounds fun." You could allow them to go past you with some curiosity, barely giving them a second thought.

Or, you could do something different. You could read them diligently. You could see them not as an idle challenge to *someone* but as a personal challenge to *you*. You could respond to that challenge by saying, "Fine, yes, challenge accepted."

You could go on an *adventure*. And perhaps, you might just end up in a fantastic story.

What will you choose?

HERE'S YOUR FIRST CHALLENGE:

Book a trip somewhere you've always wanted to go. It might be short, perhaps to a national park nearby or a local museum you've always planned on going or to a fancy restaurant. Or it could be a long trip, perhaps to Buenos Aires, Tokyo, or yes, even Paris.

What it *must* be is somewhere *new*. Why? Because mostly we go to the same places: our office, our house, our normal restaurants. There's nothing wrong with that, but it rarely makes for a good story.

Instead, take a risk on a new destination. Look at your budget (travel can be inexpensive if you plan well), look at your calendar, and commit.

Where will *you* have your next adventure?

2

CAVES

Explore the huge system of caverns, caves and catacombs underground below Paris, left from when the Romans quarried the whole place for stone, and every once in a while a bit of Paris plunges into a hole. (From Dan K.)

～

In 1774, a street in Paris collapsed into the earth. That street no longer exists, of course, but I went to the place where it once ran. There were a few unnoteworthy shops and a dry cleaner, but when it fell into a sixty foot pit in the eighteenth century, it was called Rue D'Enfer, Street of Hell. This was *the* street to hire a prostitute or find an illicit gambling ring or lure someone to be stabbed without attracting the attention of the police.

That's why it didn't surprise me that the people of Paris went nuts when the street disappeared into a dark chasm and a dozen people died. They said the Devil himself had stretched out his malicious hand to pull the wicked down into hell. If a few people died, they probably deserved it.

This was the beginning of the Enlightenment, though, and not everyone believed the collapse was due to divine judgment, especially when a church collapsed not long afterward, killing the whole congregation.

So the king at the time, Louis XVI (remember him?), ordered a study, and what they found had more to do with the Romans, who had occupied Paris over a thousand years before, and some of the oldest buildings in Paris, than any plot of Satan.

When my audience first challenged me to explore the underground caves and catacombs of Paris, I thought it was the best adventure of any of the suggestions. I also felt that of all of them, I was the least likely to actually be able to accomplish it.

There are 170 miles of caves, secret tunnels, and catacombs beneath Paris, and most of them are illegal to walk through. In fact, the underground police who patrol the catacombs weld shut all the entrances and exits, which means you can't just walk into them, even if you knew where the entrance was.

As I researched how to get into the tunnels, though, I learned there was a secret group called the cataphiles who knew how to get in and out of the catacombs. I also learned that a few of them were willing to guide neophytes through safely, which was important because even if you do manage to find an unsealed entrance to the caves, navigating miles upon miles of twisting passages in pitch-darkness is no easy feat.

I knew I needed a cataphile if I was going to accomplish the adventure I had been challenged to. But how to find one? I didn't know anyone in Paris. I spoke no French. Why would anyone want to take me down into the catacombs?

I had only one idea. One afternoon, a few days after we

arrived in Paris, I emailed my readers, "You want me to explore the catacombs beneath Paris? Fine. But I'm going to need your help. Find me a cataphile! I don't know where you'll find one or how, but I can't explore the catacombs of Paris without one. It's up to you."

I had no expectations their search would result in anything, though. If I couldn't find anything, why would I expect their luck to be any better? So while I waited for them, I decided to see what I could do on my own. I made plans to explore one area in the caves below Paris on my own, a restaurant that had reportedly been built into a cave many meters below the city. If my audience found a cataphile for me later, even better.

It turned out to be a big mistake.

"So you don't mind watching the baby?" Talia asked.

"No! You guys go have fun," said Caroline.

"Are you sure?"

"Of course! Get out of here!" she said.

Caroline, a friend from home, was traveling for work and managed to get a fifty-hour layover in Paris. She was spending the night on our couch. For us, her visit meant two things:

1. A friend! In the two weeks we'd spent in Paris so far, we'd had almost no contact with anyone except each other and Mars, our toddler. We weren't quite *desperate* for contact with other English speakers, but we weren't *not* desperate. But even more importantly, her visit meant:

2. Free babysitting! One of the surprises about traveling in Paris with a small child was that after seven at night, we were pretty much stuck inside. Want to explore Paris at night? Tough luck, you have a baby sleeping in the room

next to you. Worse, Mars was loud, unruly, and unbelievably messy when we ate out, which meant we ate dinner at home most nights. Talia was an amazing cook, and she was learning to make all sorts of French dishes, but we still missed getting to eat out at all the great Parisian restaurants.

As we escaped the apartment that night, I felt like I had been drowning for weeks and was finally coming up for air. *THIS is what Paris is meant to be like*, I thought, *free to explore, to walk down ancient streets with the love of your life, Paris by night, the most beautiful city in the world.* I reached for Talia's hand.

"I feel bad," said Talia.

"I'm too desperate to feel bad," I said.

"It's her only night in Paris," she said.

"She got here last night. She's had more time out alone than *we've* had. Besides, she's getting a free room in Paris."

"I guess so," said Talia, who took my hand limply.

The only reservation we had been able to get was for 9:30 p.m., and so we left early and took the long way over Pont Neuf, passed La Samaritaine and took the left fork to Rue de Rivoli where we went west and then up Rue de l'Arbre Sec just a block and finally west along Rue Bailleul.

Most people go out every meal in Paris, but we couldn't even afford to go out to lunch more than once a week. I had set aside just enough money for the adventures, and that night we were having an adventure.

When we arrived on the street where the restaurant was supposed to be, we found everything shuttered up. I wondered if we were entirely in the wrong place, the wrong neighborhood, the wrong city even. We got to the end of the street without finding it and had to walk back. We almost missed it again the second time. It looked like an office with a big glass door, no sign, and a just keypad and a speaker to buzz the host stand at the end of long dark hallway. I was nervous I was still in the wrong place and we were still twenty minutes early so we walked back the way we came and found a corner café.

"*Un noisette, s'il vous plaît,*" I told the impatient waitress.

"*Café crème,*" said Talia.

As we waited for our reservation, I thought about the way these types of restaurants are intentionally intimidating with their prix fixe menus and buzz-in entrances, as if to force their would-be patrons to take a risk, to explore something wholly other and not just another mediocre French restaurant. It was all part of the show. At the same time, I knew I had been co-opted by it.

It was time. I paid for our coffees with all the coins I had been collecting. We walked back to the long dark hallway, approached the door, and pressed the buzzer. I waited, feeling like a fool, but then a young man came to the door smiling.

"Welcome to Spring," he said. "Do you have a reservation? Yes? Excellent, what is the name? Bunting. Excellent. Please follow me."

The dining room was dimly lit and loud, couples packed into the small space.

I chose Spring because the Wall Street Journal had profiled it as one of the coolest ways to experience the hidden caves and catacombs of Paris. Spring didn't just have one hidden cave; it had two. There was the basement of the restaurant, which was renovated by chef and owner Daniel Rose into a second dining room. But there was also another, even more exclusive cave, seventy-two feet below ground, and this was what I most wanted to see. I also knew that this second cave was off limits to guests, and there was little to no chance I would actually be able to see it.

But even if we weren't able to see the second cave, it would be even worse if we weren't able to sit in the first cave. As the host guided us through the restaurant I worried he was going to sit us up on the first level and not the dining cave below.

But then he turned the corner and took us down a long staircase carved out of rock and through an arch made of pale limestone blocks, and there we were, eighteen feet below the city, tucked into a corner in perhaps the most expensive cave in Paris.

Our table was between another couple who were quietly enjoying their meal and a table with two American women who looked to be mother and daughter. We were easily the youngest pair in the restaurant. In most restaurants, you are handed a menu when you sit, but at Spring, we were given just a wine list. Spring had a prix fixe menu, meaning that the whole restaurant would have the same meal, which changed once a week.

A prix fix menu is great if you're an adventurous eater who wants to try new things, but while I was certainly open to delicious food, I wouldn't exactly call myself an adventurous eater. In fact, for almost my entire life, I gagged on tomatoes, turned down any salad without ranch dressing, and wouldn't touch mussels until I was in my thirties. I ate dog in Cambodia, sure, but it was cooked well-done. Besides, I didn't have a lot to eat in Cambodia, so almost any meat was fine by me. Even so, when my fellow travellers were eating fried monkey on a stick, tarantula, and other uncomfortable foods, I said a firm, "No thank you." I like delicious food, but not *weird* food. With a prix fixe menu, though, you were at the whim of the chef, and so I had to prepare myself for anything. Probably not monkey on a stick, but who knows what else.

We ordered the second cheapest bottle of wine on the wine list (the most expensive *listed* was more than a thousand euro), and settled in to wait for the first courses to arrive. In a few minutes, a blonde server came with three little white plates.

"The chef has sent you an amuse-bouche. These are razor clams in an infused chile sauce with cilantro," she said, pointing with her pinky at a long, thin seashell with chunks of white meat that must have been the razor clam—I had never seen one before. It was sitting in a thin orange sauce and had long slices of green cilantro.

"Here we have smoked venison with ground pear jam," she said, pointing to a smattering of dark red meat and light green drizzle.

"And last," she pointed to wafer-thin pears, "we have sliced pears in olive oil and ground peppercorn."

First, I had no idea what an amuse-bouche is.

Second, venison? As in deer? I like my deer in the woods or, at the very most, dead on the side of the road. But at an ultra-fancy restaurant? Hmm . . . .

I slowly pierced a piece of the "clams" with my fork and lifted it to my mouth. A smooth, spicy punch. Delicious.

Next, I tasted a bit of the venison. And it was amazing. Warm, soft, sweet, savory.

Last, I tried the pears, which were crisp and sweet, with just a bit of pop from the peppercorn.

I still didn't know what an amuse-bouche was—Talia later explained they're little treats sent by the chef, to *amuse* I assumed—but it was an amazing first impression.

By the time the first "real" course came around, we were already a glass of wine in, and after not eating since noon, we were very hungry.

"We have seared scallops with asparagus carpaccio, artichoke heart, mackerel, and mint." The dish looked beautiful, sure, but the tiny silver fish were stressful. I had never been into anchovies on pizza—had never even tried them—to be honest, and yet here they were, unavoidable, tucked into every part of my dish. I was starving, but I was also unprepared for this.

And yet, each dish was costing us thirty dollars, which we didn't really have, and I was going to eat it! I took a bite of seared scallop and mackerel and a bit of artichoke heart. It melted in my mouth. The scallops were cooked perfectly and had an earthy softness to them. The artichoke heart tossed in mint gave it a tangy bite and I barely noticed that tiny little fish except for the yummy savoriness it gave the whole bite. I loved it so much.

By the second course we were enjoying ourselves. Perhaps it was the wine or maybe it was the cave, but I wanted to eat like this every night. This was luxury. This was living! Every sense was attuned. When the couple beside us got the next course I was jealous of them that they got to eat so much deliciousness, but also sad for us because we were almost halfway done!

"For our second course we have poached sole with button mushrooms, kumquat, and fried leeks in a foie gras and broth stew."

Foie gras? We were really hitting all the disgusting parts now, weren't we, Daniel Rose, you son of a bok choy. And yet, my first bite was sweet tang of early-spring kumquats, the bitter crunch of leeks, the complex savoriness of goose liver stew, and the melt-in-your-mouthiness of the fish. It was such a bright, singing dish and I couldn't believe how much I was loving all the things I would have otherwise been too terrified to try.

By this point, we were having an amazing experience.

This was what Paris was about. Decadent food, a beautiful woman, delicious wine, all in a centuries-old setting. The room echoed with my joy.

"Our main course is filet of boeuf with tube parsnips, caramelized shallots, and a bone marrow au jus. Enjoy!"

It was tender and buttery and we groaned as we ate it.

After an hour of eavesdropping, I had realized that the two women beside us were an American mother and daughter living in Paris. The daughter had some kind of architectural firm and they spent most of the dinner talking about money and real estate and the stock market. They didn't smile or seem to enjoy the food, but they also gave the restaurant an air of sophistication, and I imagined myself with enough money to live in Paris and eat at, for me, poverty-inducing restaurants regularly enough that they no longer impressed me. I imagined their husbands or ex-husbands and how satisfied and stable and cold it would be to live like that, and I both longed for that life and felt pity for them.

But now the dessert was here and all of our neighbors had paid their bills and left. It was nearly midnight and we were satiated and thrilled but growing sleepy when the server approached with our final plates.

"For dessert we have pineapple-cilantro sorbet. This is a coconut cream puff and Italian citrus brûlée tart. Last, we have sautéed bananas in a spiced-rum sauce." And it was all delicious and fit so perfectly into everything we had eaten, and plus there were four plates of dessert, so how could we complain, how to feel anything but grateful?

But the meal was nearly finished and there was one thing I wanted still, one thing I knew I would regret if I didn't see. I also knew I was far too embarrassed to ask.

But then Talia asked our server to take our picture. We

had been chatting with her for the whole almost-three-hour meal, so she felt like a long-lost friend. After our picture, I stayed next to the staircase that led down to the cellar and I asked her about the cave. She gave me the usual P.R. pitch that I already knew and then she said the perfect six words. "Do you want to see it?"

"Sure, that would be great," I said calmly, but inside I was jumping up and down like a child.

We descended a staircase that took us almost two stories down and then we were in the cave. There were hams hanging from the ceiling and on a table were giant wheels of cheese. On the walls were racks filled with thousands of bottles of wine. The floor was soft and I looked down and realized it was fine gravel, not smooth cement. I was below even the sewers of Paris, as low as the catacombs, I could feel the depth in that room, the quietness of the limestone walls, and the amazing smells of the food.

It was enchanting, and I was surprised by my good luck to even be there. At the same time, I thought about how tiny this was compared to the secret and illegal tunnels, the catacombs. I was accomplishing my first adventure, and yet it felt so empty without the real catacombs.

We talked to the server for a few more moments and then we went up, out of the restaurant, back onto Rue de Bailleul, which no longer felt unfriendly. And we walked across the river and back to Rue des Canettes, up the stairs, into our flat, where we found our sleeping baby and a jetlagged Caroline.

In bed, I put my arm around Talia, who stirred up close to me. She was already asleep but would have woken if I pressed her. But the baby was there and Caroline in the other room and I knew neither of us would have enjoyed it,[1] so I turned over and checked my email on my phone. There was one from Arlen, one of my readers, with the subject line, "Cataphile."

"I've found you a cataphile," he wrote. "Joe, meet David Aubert, David Aubert, meet Joe. Joe, he has agreed to take you into the catacombs."

I had found my cataphile. I had never felt closer to a book. I could almost smell the ink of the publishing contract.

~

Challenge no. 2: Dark

Dark places are everywhere; you just don't think about it. Your closet is often a good one. Under a thick blanket is a second best option. If you're feeling very brave and adventurous, google the closest cave for spelunking.

Then, put yourself in a dark place for five minutes. Set a timer. Then shut down your phone. Turn off your flashlight and sit there, in the dark, for five minutes. How does it feel to be shut off from the sense you are likely *most* connected to? Are you scared? Are you excited? Or even bored? Observe your feelings.

Then emerge back into the light. How does it feel to be out of the dark?

3

DIRECTIONS

Select a destination (any destination) in Paris and see if you can find your way there using only the locals for help. You must speak only French! (From Kate F.)

∾

B ack in the States, whenever I told people I was going to Paris, there was always a fifty-fifty chance they would feel sorry for me.

"Paris is great, but the French are the worst." They would look at me in deep concern, as if to say, "Oh . . . you bought into that Francophile lie? I'm so sorry that you're going to waste your time in that horrible place."

What almost always followed was a story of their bad treatment at the hands of a Parisian, as if their entire opinion of Paris, and the country of France, was formed for the sole reason of being able to tell their story of a rude waiter or a person who purposefully gave them the wrong directions during their three-day-long visit to Paris.

Not to overgeneralize, but I also found that those who

had bad experiences were much more likely to be loud and from Florida. Nothing against loud Floridians. Loud Floridians are great. But they seem to be incompatible with the shy, entitled French.

I believe *that*, more than anything, was why my audience responded so much to my next adventure, because it was meant to act as a kind of vaccination against this vision of the French as rotten and rude.

This challenge was to get to a destination using only the locals for help, and speaking French. It was given to me by a thirteen-year-old girl from Pennsylvania who I'm sure was laughing at the thought of me, a shy American writer, stammering his Google'd French to beret-wearing art historians all sipping tiny cups of espresso with their pinkies up.

Thanks, Kate. Thanks a lot.

But the adventure was seconded by a woman with more altruistic motives.

"As a Parisian," she said, "I would like for your experience to prove that you can actually stumble upon some very helpful people! Good luck working on your French!"

But there was the problem: the French language.

There are many things I detest about myself, but I would place my inability to learn any language in the top fifty, maybe even top twenty-five.

I had, of course, learned a few French phrases before we left. I had tried, and failed, many times to read *Le Petit Prince* to Mars. However, the pronunciation of French is intimidating. And by intimidating, I mean the only way I knew how to pronounce anything in that country was by listening to the online translation lady say the same word a thousand times on repeat.

I knew the French are persnickety about their pronunciation. I honestly worried no one would be able to understand what I was saying, and I would get lost. Worse, if I did get lost, I wouldn't just be leading my own stupid self astray, but also my wife, Talia, our toddler, and a leather messenger bag filled with all my shame.

Yeah. Thanks, Kate. This is going to be *so* fun.

As MISERABLE AS this adventure was, it was still a miracle we were even there.

The town where Talia and I had lived before Paris had just one distinction: it was the chicken capital of the world. More chickens are slaughtered in that ten mile radius than any other. You drive down the main road into town with its wide lawns and beautiful plantation-style houses and get stuck at a light behind a semi truck towering with cages filled with thousands of huddled chickens heading to the slaughterhouse. Worse than the smell is the knowledge that you're looking at tonight's dinner.

Never in my life had I dreamed I would live in the American South, and certainly not a small town in the foothills of the Appalachian mountains, but I did find myself living there for five years, two of which were the best of my life and three of which were filled with increasing desperation.

I was born and grew up in Santa Barbara, California, which is arguably the most beautiful place in the world. However, there were things even Santa Barbara was short of: seasons, tall trees, rivers, and most especially, for me anyway, a certain girl who after just one coffee date I found myself reorienting my world for, as if I had been walking on the clouds my whole life and had discovered gravity was drawing my feet to the earth.

While we were still dating, Talia and I talked about our visions for our future lifestyle.

"A writer needs to travel," I said. "I want to live in a new place every six months."

Talia got quiet. Talia was never quiet. I felt my stomach drop.

"Um. Are you okay?" I said.

"I never want to do that, Joe. I can't just pick up and go live somewhere else every six months. I need a home."

It became one of those unresolvable fights that we would come back to every few months, but it was a fight I was losing. Because for four years, I had lived in that small town, not traveling, not complaining, trying to embrace our lives there. When Mars was born, it made leaving that much harder. We signed a lease on a larger apartment, locking us in for another year at least. I tried to make the most of it. But I couldn't help longing for a new city, a new walk, a new life. That wanderlust was on me, like a fever. I felt it constricting my chest and pressing against the bones of my face. I wanted to be gone from that place. I had no way of getting out of that place.

One night, after writing all day on a project I didn't care about, I drove home in the rain. It had been the rainiest spring Georgia had seen in a hundred years. Just a few months before, the whole state had been in the worst drought in a decade. The lake had been so low the banks stretched down thirty feet to the water. There was more mud than lake. But that night, as I drove home, I looked over to see the water up to the trunks of the red oaks and tulip poplars crowding around the lake. It never stopped raining.

Or was that the year before? I couldn't remember, and what else could that be but a sign of just how lost I had been. I had been going through the motions. The seasons had blurred together. The years had become indistinguishable. I needed to get out of there.

Pulling up to my parking spot in our apartment complex, I had rushed through the rain into our tiny two-bedroom unit. It was a mess, as usual. There were leaves by the door, tracked in from the porch. Piles of pots and pans were left unwashed on the counter. Mars stared at me guiltily from the floor with my best books and my collection of *New Yorker*s strewn around him. Talia was sitting on the couch on her phone, her feet up, playing the latest game she was obsessed with.

For the previous four months, this had been my life: pushing aside my writing to hold a crying infant. On my writer's "salary" and Talia's nonprofit job, we couldn't afford childcare. So she worked mornings, I worked afternoons, and we both worked nights. Our system sort of worked, but after four months of long days and depressed productivity, I had reached a breaking point.

I wanted to be a writer. I wanted to travel and write books and publish articles read by thousands of people all over the world. And I had done all of that. I had written books. My website, thewritepractice.com, where I taught writing, had been read by over a million people that year. And yet, when I went home to my disgusting apartment in a chicken-infested town, to my wife more interested in her smartphone than in me,[1] to my son systematically destroying all my favorite things, I didn't feel much like a real writer.

The answer was escape. The answer was Paris. In Paris I would be able to write. I imagined what it would feel like to hold my own book in my hand, my own name in raised letters. The thought of it felt like a bell ringing through my sternum.

God, I need to get out of this place, I thought. *How do I get out of this place?*

"We have to leave soon," said Talia, without looking up from her phone.

"What are you talking about?" I said.

"My brother's party, remember?" I hadn't remembered, of course. "Neil is bringing his new girlfriend."

"Oh. Right," I said. "Hey, so remember how we talked about Grandma getting married in Florence?"

"Is she actually getting married?" asked Talia.

"Who knows with Grandma."

"True. And either way it will be fun to go for her eighty-fifth birthday."

"Right. Anyway, I was thinking, what if we stayed there afterward?" I said, trying to keep my voice even.

"What do you mean?"

"I just figure, the expensive part is the plane tickets. We could go early and stay in Europe for a few months, maybe in Paris."

"I love Paris." She looked up from her phone. Talia's eyes have this golden color to them, and just at that moment they were shining.

"I know you do."

"Could we afford it?"

"I don't know. I think so."

"What about my job?"

"You might have to quit your job."

"That seems really risky. What about the baby, though?"

"I've always wanted to try traveling with kids."

"I don't know. Ugh, I'm getting panicky."

"I think it could be really great."

"Can we talk about something else? This is giving me anxiety."

I fed Mars while Talia got ready for the party. Feeding a six-month-old is always something like a Jackson Pollock painting, globs of sweet potato dripping onto the table and high chair and most of all onto the baby. Mars liked to grab the spoon and wave it around, ensuring half the food ended up in his stomach, the other half on his face, in his hair, and on the floor. We put down a towel for a drop cloth which is how all of our towels got ruined. And the whole time, I would just stare at him, waiting while he took his next painstakingly slow bite, doing my best to get as much of the food as possible in his stomach and not everywhere else and realizing all the while my best was never good enough. By the time Talia was ready to leave, Mars had a foo-manchu mustache made of sweet potato and slobber.

We took the long driveway, near pitch black in the rainy weather, down to Talia's brother's lake house. I saw the lights on through the giant windows, could almost feel the warmth coming from inside. Talia's brother lived in a modernist bachelor pad looking out on the woods and the long stretch of black water of Lake Lanier below. Every morning he would go out on the dock at the bottom of the hill and drink his coffee, journal, and look out at the lake in the morning mist. He took kayaks from there, too, and would ride into the inlets and to the little islands dotting the lake for long picnics on the rocky red banks, and in the summers we would meet there and grill meat on the patio and drink cheap beer and lounge and laugh in the wet Georgia heat. Even when we brought Mars, I was relaxed there.

When we parked, Talia ran inside with the baby while I got out the supplies: pack-n-play, blankets, onesie pajamas, sleep sack, pacifiers, stuffed animal. I took it all downstairs and set it up in a quiet room and then put Mars down and he went right to sleep.

As I walked back up the stairs, I thought, I could be okay

with this. I could learn to be happy here. It might take me years, but I could do it.

When I came up Talia was talking to Neil and his new girlfriend. Neil is one of our best friends, as steady and stable a man as you'll ever meet.

I could be like Neil, I thought. I could go to work every day and save my paycheck and every once in a while go do a trip somewhere for a week and then I'll go back to the routine and I'll be happy. Neil is a good man and I could be like Neil. I could be happy, right? I will be happy. I will. I will.

"Oh did I tell you we're going to Paris?" Talia told them. "Yeah! Joe's grandma is getting married in Florence and we're going to go a few months early and live in Paris. Yeah, it's going to be amazing. We're really excited."

Typical Talia.

I walked up next to her and I put my hand on her back and I kissed her cheek.

"We're so excited," I said.

I HAD INVITED Talia on the directions adventure, thinking this would be the perfect time to introduce her and Mars to these adventures. Maybe it would make for a fun family adventure.

Talia didn't see it that way. Talia oscillates between anxiety and enthusiasm. I knew any of these adventures would trigger that anxiety, but I figured a nice walk to a garden cemetery wouldn't be that bad.

"Let's just do this and get it over with," she said when we left the apartment. I guess I overestimated the allure of a nice walk.

"Come on! This is great! We're doing it! We're in Paris! Going on an adventure! You should be excited!"

She gave me a look that reminded me of some of the faces I'd seen in pictures of the catacombs and so I gave up trying to be her cheerleader.

To be honest, I felt the same way. If Dante was right and there are seven layers of hell, traveling with a jet lagged baby is like being trapped one level up from Satan himself. I was jet lagged. I was sleep deprived. Most of all, I felt exposed, as if Paris was about to reveal me as a fraud. The idea of being out in the city all day with a toddler and no map felt terrifying, like being stuck out in the desert sun with no water.

These are the things you don't hear about in the travel guides or your friends' Facebook posts: how uncomfortable travel can be, how much easier it can be to stay home in your hotel room or your rented flat, how tempting it is to go to the proven restaurants and clichéd attractions, how hard it can be for so many of us to talk to strangers who speak a strange language.

I don't want you to think I'm whining when I talk about this, or that I'm trying to create drama out of nothing. After all, I was in Paris. I should have been happy! But the reality is that travel wears on you, especially when you're trying intentionally to seek adventure and not the usual sights and tastes of most other tourists.

And so it was that we walked out of our flat on a sunny afternoon in Paris completely miserable, annoyed with each other, our trip, and with Paris itself.

I was not unprepared, though. In fact, I was probably overprepared.

My secret to surviving a day without a map[2], with only the goodwill of strangers, my least favorite people group, was preparation. This looked like reading and re-reading the back of our guidebook, that section with all the travel phrases. I also spent a lot of time searching for articles on the etiquette of approaching random people on the streets in Paris. Didn't have much luck there. And, of course, I spent many hours sitting on the floor, my head in my hands, flipping between panic and grief: "Why me? Why did *I* have to be the one to make a fool of myself in the most sophisticated city in the world?" The whole adventure seemed, in my stress-addled brain, to be something like dying, which I know is a little melodramatic, but it's how I felt. I might indeed make it through talking to strangers, I thought, but if I did, I would have entered a different world. I would be a different person.

However, in between my anxiety attacks, I was making progress.

WE WALKED up Boulevard Saint Germain. My strategy was to stand near the metro station and ask a stranger for directions there since that would put us right next to the best mode of transportation to get across the city.

I did not *want* to talk to strangers. I *had* to talk to strangers. I wanted to find an excuse *out* of talking to strangers. There *was* no way out of talking to strangers.

Here we go.

We got to the corner by the metro stop, and I stood there. I stood there and waited. People walked past me. I tried to make eye contact. No one looked at me. I tried to will myself to reach out and stop someone. I failed.

After a few minutes of standing there like a street preacher who had lost his voice, I realized this wasn't working

"This is the wrong spot," I said, half to Talia, half to my

bruised ego. "People here are too busy. Let's go to the next stop, down the street. It's a little more touristy and less crowded. I think it will be easier to ask someone directions there."

We walked down Saint Germain to the Odeon stop.

I saw two old men standing on the corner. They looked friendly enough, both impeccably dressed in sport coats and dress pants. One wore a hat, the other a vest. If I couldn't talk to them I couldn't talk to anyone. But I was starting to think I couldn't talk to *anyone*. This was way too hard. I was supposed to be on vacation here, or workation at least, and yet I was here on the corner, my hands shaking as I pushed Mars, all because I couldn't talk to a stranger. Hemingway would never have been this nervous. Even Fitzgerald, with all his neuroses, would have gone up to them smiling, lit a cigarette and then started a conversation that would have inevitably led to them escorting him through the city and thanking him for the honor. I was the worst at this.

I began to walk up to them, pushing Mars in his stroller. Then stopped, pulled out my phone to pretend to check the time, watching them out of the corner of my eye. They were still there, chatting amiably. I thought about turning around and giving up. This was so stupid. Why was I doing these adventures anyway? Then Mars turned his head and looked up at me, and in his blue eyes I realized I couldn't turn back.

"Excusez-muah," I said. I caught them in mid-conversation and they glanced up at me. I plowed forward. "Pouvez-vous me dire où Père Lachaise, s'il vos plaît?"

"Comment?" said the man in the vest, now turning toward me.

"Pouvez-vous me dire où Père Lachaise cimetière?"

"Père Lachaise?"

"Oui, Père Lachaise?"

"Ah . . ." they spoke in rapid French to each other. I had no idea what they were saying, but I was hopeful for the first time.

Then, they nodded vigorously, as if they had come to a consensus. The man in the vest started talking to me in French.

"Oh, désolé," I said. "Parle vous anglais? Mon Francais est mauvais."

"English?" he asked.

I nodded.

"Ah, oui, yes, for Père Lachaise take the metro." He said the word metro beautifully, *meh-trough*. I loved hearing them speak, these old French men.

"Désolé, which metro line? And which stop?"

He walked me to a big map just beside the metro stop and gestured to a metro stop on the 3 line called Pére Lachaise.

"You take the 4 line from here, Odeon," he explained, "and you get off at Réaumur and transfer to 3 line there and you go three-four-five-six stops to Père Lachaise."

He was very kind, and his friend in the hat stood there squinting up at the map and nodding along, grunting things I didn't understand in French.

I felt slightly guilty that he was speaking such fluent English and I wasn't insisting we use French, but it seemed more rude to correct him. After all, my French was *mauvais*, his English was *très bien*, and I didn't want to force him to listen to me butcher his language while he spoke mine so beautifully.

After he explained the route—he actually explained it two or three times—I asked his name.

"Joseph," he said.

"Joseph? That's my name! I'm Joe. Wow. Very nice to meet you."

"You are from America?"

"Yes, from California . . . and Georgia."

"My niece lives in New Jersey," he said.

"Oh, very nice. My sister lives there. There are nice parts and not so nice parts. I hope your daughter lives in the nice part."

We talked for several minutes more about America and Paris and how long we were staying and what we thought of it so far. He was very nice. I met his friend too, Phillipe, the man in the hat. Philippe didn't have an American niece and so didn't speak English as well.

I left the conversation beaming, feeling like Paris was open to me, the whole city was there for me, for *me*, and all I had to do was reach out and embrace it.

If I could just remember *this*, I thought, this feeling of acceptance, of connection to these people and this city, then perhaps life would be easier in Paris and I *would* actually finish these adventures. I was only working on my second now, but I was already feeling like I would never finish. But if I could just remember this moment, then perhaps I would have the energy to finish, perhaps even make it to the real catacombs.

I was thinking of all of these things when we promptly got lost.

WE CAME up to the staircase to the metro Joseph had pointed us to, but stairs are difficult with a stroller. So we took Mars out, folded it up, and carried him down the stairs.

Except we couldn't get down the stairs to the metro; people kept blocking our way, and we found ourselves walking against a crowd of people. When we finally got to the bottom of the staircase the way was blocked by a big metal gate.

Where was the entrance?

"Bonjour, puis-je vous aider?" said a pretty young woman who was coming out of the exit.

"Bonjour . . . um . . . parle vous anglais?" I said.

"Yes. Can I help you? Are you trying to go to the metro?" she said.

"Yes, thank you. I guess we went the wrong way."

"It's okay. I will show you." She walked us to the correct staircase a few paces away. "Is this your first time visiting Paris?"

"My first time," I said. "My wife has been here . . . three times?" Talia nodded and smiled.

"How do you like it so far?" The street was crowded and she walked beside us, guiding us toward the right stop.

"It's a beautiful city," I said. "We're going to Père Lachaise cemetery. My friends challenged us to get there without using a map, just asking for directions from Parisians."

"I think you will find many people to help you," she said, a kind smile on her face, and in that moment, I couldn't help but love this city.

"I hope so. Thank you so much for your help!"

After we made it on that first train, getting to the Père Lachaise stop was simple enough. Just as Joseph suggested, we changed trains at Réaumur-Sébastopol. A few stops later was Père Lachaise. When we made it back up to the street, now miles from where we started, I was about to ask for directions for a third time when I saw a sign pointing to the cemetery. I walked with Talia along an old stone wall and then carried the stroller up a worn staircase and found myself in Père Lachaise.

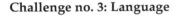

Challenge no. 3: Language

Find a place where they speak another language. Perhaps it's your local Mexican market (my favorite), a French adult-ed class, or even an online chat room for Bulgarians.

Practice a few phrases before hand (like the ones listed). Then, jump into the conversation. How did it go?

5 Useful French Phrases for Getting Directions in Paris

How then *do* you approach random strangers in Paris to ask for directions? It's really not as hard as I was feeling it was.

So if you, dear reader, ever get lost in Paris without a smartphone, here are a few French phrases you can use to ask for help.

1. *Excusez-moi*
Rough pronunciation: ess-cuse-ay mwah
Translation: Excuse me.
When to use it: In Paris, good manners are essential, especially when interrupting strangers to ask for help. You're relying on their goodwill (i.e. to give you directions to where you ask, not to the train station with a note to the ticket office asking them to sell you a ticket out of town!).

I received kind treatment from many strangers and part of the reason is because I said *excusez-moi* before asking for help.

2. *Parlez-vous Anglais?*

Rough pronunciation: par-leh voo ahng-glae

Translation: Do you speak English?

When to use it: This is an essential tip for those who want to show the French respect, and thus receive better treatment at their hands.

This is the easy way out if you're not confident enough in your traveller's French to ask for directions. The temptation might be to simply ask this in English, but you'll get much better results and much kinder treatment if you respect the local language enough to ask in French.

If you'd rather soldier on with your French and ask for directions directly, then skip to the next phrase.

Note that while most Parisians speak at least some English—and speak it much better than most Americans speak French—many Parisians will say no when you ask them this question. However, usually, as you try to use your bad French, they will interrupt you and speak in English.

3. *Comment puis-je arriver à* __[Cimetière du Père Lachaise]__ (insert your destination).

Rough pronunciation: cohm-ahn pweez-jeh ah-reve-air ah __[your destination]__).

Translation: How do you get to __[Cimetière du Père Lachaise]__ (insert your destination)?

When to use it: As in English, there are many ways to ask for directions to a place, but to me, this was the one that sounded most natural and was easiest to pronounce.

However, I've also included a few more below. First, though, let's go over a few other phrases that will be helpful in asking for directions.

·   ·   ·

4. *Désolé, mon français est mauvais.*

Rough pronunciation: Dez-olay, mahn frah-say eh mah-vay.

Translation: Sorry, my French is bad!

When to use it: We used this phrase constantly. Talia especially was fond of it. When you use it, most French will quickly take pity on you and respond very kindly if you show this respectful unfamiliarity with their beloved language.

5. *Pouvez-vous me dire où est* __[Cimetière du Père Lachaise]__ (insert your destination)?

Rough pronunciation: poo-vay voo meh deer oo eh cemeh-teer doo Pair Leh-chase?

Translation: Can you direct me to __[Cimetière du Père Lachaise]__ (insert your destination)?

When to use it: This seems to be a bit more formal than number three. It's also a little easier to pronounce, so this is the one I relied on.

OTHER WORDS and Phrases You Might Need

C'est loin d'ici? Is it far from here?

Désolé, pouvez-vous répéter? Sorry, can you repeat that?

Quel est votre nom? What is your name?

Gauche. Left.

Droit. Right.

Un, deux, trois, quatre, cinq, six, sept, huit, neuf, dix. One through ten.

4

PÈRE LACHAISE

Père Lachaise Cimetiere awaits you. Hunt down the grave sites of Molière, Richard Wright, Balzac, Proust and Colette, commune with their ghosts and leave a flower at each. Over a million people are buried there, some on 30 year leases. Sorry to say, you can no longer leave kisses in red lipstick on Oscar Wilde's monument, as it is encased in a protective covering; or spend the night at Jimmy Morrison's grave, as it is guarded now by bouncers. Even so, it's fun to watch others try! (From Julia W.)

~

I t was at the first grave, Gertrude Stein's, that I realized why I needed these adventures.

Since I first considered Paris, I had been looking forward to the cafés. Coffee, wine, atmosphere, writing, people watching—it was like a mantra for all my expectations of Paris. I expected it to lead to a personal renaissance, a burst of creativity unmatched thus far in my life. And yet most of the time when I went to the cafés to write I couldn't get anything out.

Paris was cold in March and one day I went to the café down the street from our apartment. I sat down beside a man with an I <3 Amsterdam lighter who was drinking whiskey. I ordered coffee and when the waiter brought it to me, I finished it in just a moment. It was cold and I wanted another but I couldn't afford it.

"What shall I write about?" I wrote. "Where is my story? Is this my story? Where is it? I'm lost."

There you are, in the most inspiring place in the world. You know you should be writing, but it won't come out. There's too much pressure. No one can live up to the standard of Paris. You worry you will never write again.

It smelled like cigarettes and the waiter's cologne. There were four Americans talking loudly nearby, which made me cringe, but then I wondered if I only thought they were talking loudly because they were the only ones I could understand.

You do not feel more alive while writing in a cafe in Paris. You do not even feel more awake, although the cold helps. What you feel is more distracted. The old questions are still there, but there is so much going on that you can't help but stop thinking about it for a few moments.

The problem with writing an adventure memoir in Paris is that Parisians are not very adventurous. You can sip champagne from the Eiffel Tower, but can't bungee jump. You can find the most amazing cheeses and sausages that melt in your mouth like candy, but you can't raft down the Seine. You can ride a bike and rollerblade with ten thousand other Parisians, but you can't stay out past one in the morning because that's when the bars close.

I needed the adventures. I would never have gone to Père Lachaise without them; I would never have stood in front of the grave of Gertrude Stein, mentor to Hemingway. I was finding my way through the cemetery, and through it, finding my own story.

PÈRE LACHAISE WAS PARIS' first "garden cemetery." It was beautiful, cemetery or not, with tall shady trees and cobblestone streets that made pushing Mars' stroller a long, slow affair.

I laid the first rose on Gertrude Stein's grave. Stein was a modernist poet, bestselling memoirist, and Ernest Hemingway's once-writing mentor. Stein led a group of expat writers and artists in the 1920s that she called the Lost Generation. It was just after World War I, and the social structures and moral codes that had held society together had been killed in so many ways in the trenches of Normandy.

Paris in the 1920s was an amazing place, filled with some of the greatest artists of the twentieth century (which, if you've seen *Midnight in Paris*, you understand). Among writers, there were T.S. Eliot, James Joyce, the poet Ezra Pound, Ernest Hemingway, and F. Scott Fitzgerald, who had just published a unique novel that was unfortunately selling poorly. It was called *The Great Gatsby*, and after reading it, Hemingway was so inspired that he decided that his next writing project *had* to be a novel.

Stein was at the center of this Parisian group of artist expats. She was wealthy. She owned paintings by the greatest living modernist painters alive, most of whom were living in Paris at the time. Publishers would come to her house and be so awed by the paintings that they would fall over themselves to please her and publish her writing.

Hemingway eventually had a falling out with her when, according to him, he overheard an argument she had with her partner, Alice Toklas. He had known, sort of, that she was gay before that. But then he overheard Toklas speak to her "as I had never heard one person speak to another; never, anywhere, ever," and then Stein, in response, begged, "Don't, pussy. Don't. Don't, please don't do it. Please don't. Please don't, pussy." Witnessing all this, the slight and the begging, made him lose all respect for her, and he stopped seeing her.

Toklas outlived Stein by twenty years, living mostly off of her writing, including a cookbook that has perhaps the first recipe for marijuana brownies. She died in 1967 and was buried next to Stein with her name engraved on the back of Stein's tombstone, perhaps the only lesbian couple burried together in Père Lachaise.

We found Stein and Toklas' grave in the middle of a long straight row toward the center of the cemetery. We left each a white rose.

Next was Honoré de Balzac. I had read a few stories by Balzac but never his longer, more famous novels. He lived in Paris in the early 1800s and was the son of a wealthy lawyer who wanted Honoré to follow him into law. Instead, he decided to become a writer—how did that conversation go, I wondered—living first in a garrett in Paris and then in more and more luxurious homes as his fortunes rose. He was friends with Victor Hugo, who was pallbearer at his funeral and gave his eulogy. As a writer, he was prolific but obsessive in his habits. He would lock himself in his house for days or even weeks to focus on his writing projects, and wrote there until he would emerge pale from sunlessness carrying a finished manuscript. We found his grave on a hill along a narrow path. It was topped by a bronze bust made by Rodin. We left a rose to his memory.

Oscar Wilde's grave had a glass wall around it because too many people had climbed it to leave bright red lipstick kisses on the tombstone. The glass case didn't do much. It too was covered in ruby lips, but the more intrepid Wilde fans—hero to many, including me—found a way over the fence to lay their lips directly on Wilde's resting place. There was even a beautiful stone angel above the grave holding a trumpet whose mouth bore the lipstick of a thousand strangers.

Oscar Wilde is one of my favorite writers. His use of language was perfect, crisp and beautiful and precise. He was funny and sad and moral and he told Shakespearian stories in a way that still seems modern and fresh today. He also lived at a time when being gay could get you arrested or even killed and managed to be authentic even at great personal risk—a risk that was realized when he was put on trial for "gross indecency" and exiled from England.

I'm not sure I could have been friends with Hemingway, too brash and always fishing and hunting and boxing. I think I could have been friends with Fitzgerald, at least for a while, but he was so opulent, so enraptured in his own fame, so distracted by Zelda and her mood swings that I can't imagine him being a very good friend. Oscar and I, though, we could have been buds. His grave was easily the most unique and beautiful we visited, perhaps the most beautiful in all of Père Lachaise, and I wanted an excuse to linger there.

I tossed a white rose over the glass fence. We left for the next grave.

Molière's grave was in a quiet section of the cemetery, a

raised stone tomb set upon four pillars and fenced in by a ring of sharp stakes. Molière was the pen name of Jean-Baptise Poquelin, one of the greatest French playwrights of all time. He wrote during the reign of Louis XIV, the Sun King of France, and his plays were performed for Louis' court. He was performing one of the characters in his final play, *The Imaginary Invalid*, when, suffering from tuberculosis, he had a coughing fit in the middle of the performance. He continued, though, completing the play, and then collapsed. He died shortly after. I set a white rose on the fence around his grave to honor his humor and courage.

We found Proust's grave next, in the northeast corner of the cemetery. It was a low marble slab scattered with flowers, so that when I put my single white rose underneath his name embossed in gold letters, the rose looked small and insufficient next to the bouquets and pots piled atop the grave. I have a fondness for Proust, more because of his personality than his writing. I'm embarrassed to say that I've never read Proust. I've scanned a few pages, but it never captivated me. Still, he was an interesting person: incredibly shy, filled with anxiety, often sick, unable to experience much of life. He lived with his parents for almost all of his life, and then died as a shut-in while he worked on his final novel. He had so little actual experience, and yet he was a deeply observant person. Yes, I will read Proust. I just need to psych myself up for it.

The last grave we visited was Jim Morrison's, and it was by far the most popular, which sounds strange to say at a cemetery, but truly, at Père Lachaise, Jim Morrison's grave is the main attraction. I first guessed we were close to it when a tall young man with a mane of dreadlocks and baggy black clothes turned onto the path just ahead of us. His smell, which we caught even walking ten feet behind him, was like incense and soil, like marijuana smells after it's grown stale. When we got near the grave we heard someone playing instrumental Asian-fusion music on a cheap stereo. A group of twenty people were milling around a police barricade that kept us all about ten feet away from a simple tombstone with the name of the mythic rock icon stamped in Roman letters. There was incense burning. It was a strange assortment of people: a woman in black jeans and a white shirt, both strategically ripped; a couple who looked like a slightly cleaned up, matured version of the sixties; several regular tourists, some in jeans and old t-shirts and some in business casual clothes; and of course our dread-maned friend standing in the back looking somber at his hero's resting place. I waded to the front of the crowd and set my rose inside the barricade, took a last look, and then left the grave and wheeled the stroller out of Père Lachaise.

"WHAT IS THE ANSWER?" Gertrude Stein asked her partner, Alice Toklas, before she died.

"There is no answer," Toklas said.

"Then there is no question," said Stein.

If not for these adventures, I would have been still been alone in a café, avoiding the gaping hole of my own lack of creativity, asking, "Where is my story? Is this really all there is? Is this it?"

Instead, I stood across from Gertrude Stein with my son and my wife, and I placed a white rose on her grave and thought, *There is no question. You do not need to know the answer to the question, Joe. You do not need to know where your story is. There is no question. You just need to live it, and to write it down. The rest will come as it always has before. There is no question.*

~

Challenge no. 4: The Dead

Visit a local cemetery. While there google the names you see on your phone. Who lived there? What is their story? What can you learn from them?

5

PAINTING

Visit an art supply shop, and buy some watercolors and quality paper. Paint a picture yourself. Then head over to the Pont des Arts and set up a crate or table and try to sell them! (From Julia W.)

We had settled into a routine in Paris. In the morning, Talia would wake up an hour before anyone else and sit at our small breakfast table to read and journal. At around six-thirty, Mars would wake up and "cuddle" with me for thirty minutes or so, which really meant crawl all over me for fifteen minutes and then wreak havoc in our apartment for another fifteen. After summoning enough energy and/or frustration I would drool myself out of bed, fetch Mars breakfast, and then take a long shower. Eventually Talia would bang on the door or Mars would crawl in with the broom between his teeth and I would be forced to *actually* begin my day.

There was no privacy in our apartment, no escape. We

had given Mars the only bedroom because anything would wake him up, especially his parents' breathing. Talia and I slept on the pull-out couch in the living room/kitchen/dining area. Imagine sleeping in your kitchen. Would that be a restful experience for you? But these are the things we do to experience culture.

After finding the outfit that would embarrass me the least on the streets of Paris where everyone dressed like off-duty barons and baronettes, I kissed Mars and Talia good-bye. Talia would look at me resentfully and give only the briefest of kisses, my daily, "You're leaving me with *this* mess?"

Then I would walk up Rue des Canettes which was still waking up with the waiters and shopkeepers only beginning to arrive and then down Rue du Four which turns into Rue de Babylone, past Berluti with all the beautiful Italian suits and Café Coton where I often fogged up the glass and Hermès and Le Bon Marché and finally to Coutume, the little café with large windows and good coffee where I would try to write my book.

You either won't believe this or already know this, but Paris has famously bad coffee. It is murky and thin and bitter in all the wrong ways. Parisians themselves call it sock water. There is nothing better than sitting in a café in Paris, but I recommend ordering wine, not coffee. Coutume was started by Australians, though, so it had two benefits and one major flaw: they made great coffee and they spoke English. The latter was the flaw just as much as it was the benefit, since part of the point of coming to France was to get to know the French, and so in the afternoons I would go home for lunch and then walk to the café at the end of Rue des Canettes called Café de la Mairie which was run by stiff French waiters in wrinkled tuxedos.

After a long day of sitting on an uncomfortable stool to research my adventures and, hopefully, get a little writing in, I would walk home, which was usually in some state of baby-induced disaster. We would go for a walk then, usually up to Rue de Buci and then to the Seine. Sometimes we would attempt some adventure. But eventually we would come home and Talia would make dinner and I would put Mars to bed.

By eight o'clock the day was done. We couldn't leave to explore the city at night, at least not together because of the baby, and so I would watch a show with Talia on her computer and drink a bottle of Rhône and think about all the things I was missing out there in the city and all the writing I should be doing. I felt hemmed in and depressed and tired in the evenings. I wanted nothing more than to be out where the writers were, to be with people who were enjoying themselves, and yet I didn't know any writers in Paris and the ones I had reached out to hadn't responded to my emails.

Once during our nightly walk, we went too far and only began home after dark. It was a Saturday night and people were enjoying themselves but we were parents who needed to get their baby to bed. We walked past Shakespeare and Company bookstore and through the Latin corner where we bought mediocre crêpes and then past the Pantheon and as we walked I looked up through the warm lit windows and thought of all the people gathering there and the parties we were missing and the friends we would never make—because we spoke such bad French and because I was shy and because of our son and because I simply didn't know how to make friends from nothing in a few months. I was surrounded by people, by a beautiful city's worth of beautiful people, and yet I had never felt more alone.

It was on a night like this that Talia told me we would finally be meeting Dorian the next day.

DORIAN WAS the one friend we had in Paris, and by friend I mean was a mutual friend of someone who had introduced us over email. Dorian lived in Paris to study cooking, but she ran in similar circles and so we knew a lot of the same people, which was as close to a friend as we had.

I saw her at a table in back. Dorian had blonde hair and pale white skin and she wore a simple black shirt and black skirt that made her look unobtrusively sophisticated. She didn't smile when she saw, just made eye contact and nodded cooly.

I did my best to maneuver Mars' stroller between the tables without bumping them and spilling some poor person's tea into their lap.

"Heeeeyyyy," said Talia, hugging her. "So great to meet you in person. This is my husband, Joe."

"Hey, I'm Joe." We shook hands and hers was warm and a little damp from holding her teacup.

"Dorian." She still didn't smile.

"How's it going?" Great intro, Joe, I thought.

We sat down for the briefest of moments before Mars wrestled his way out of his stroller and started crawling across the floor. He would have crawled under tables, stopping only to lick up the crumbs from all the beautiful cakes. I caught him, though, and he started to scream as I picked him up. This was going great.

I didn't learn how to have conversations with strangers until I began working as a journalist. What you learn as a journalist is how to be curious about people. You realize that it's a learned skill, not a personality trait.

My first interview, I spoke to the star of a high school play. We sat on the grass outside the theater.

"Um . . . What do you want to tell people about the play?" I asked.

"Didn't you come with questions?" she said.

"Yes, of course. What do you want to tell people about the play?"

It was one of the most awkward conversations in my life. I don't think I ever finished that article.

After college, I got my first gig at a little newspaper in California, and I would get panic attacks whenever I had to interview someone. As a journalist, writing is only a small part of your job. Your main role is to ask questions. And to ask questions you must be curious. You learn to turn it on, your curiosity, even if you're not feeling it, and soon you realize everyone has the potential to be fascinating if you ask the right questions.

These were the questions I wanted to ask Dorian:

Why did you come to Paris?

What is your family like? How do they feel about you living in Paris?

What do your siblings do for work? Are you the black sheep of the family or the favorite daughter?

Do you like living in Paris? Have you made any friends?

What do you do in your job? Do you love it?

What are your coworkers like?

What are your favorite patisseries? Where do you go to get the best bread? Who are your favorite pastry chefs in Paris?

But Mars was going crazy, squirming and screaming. The grannies and hipsters were looking around at us.

"Excuse me for a minute." Dorian barely glanced at me as I carried Mars out.

We walked around the long block and I told Mars about what it means to be a good friend and when I came back Talia was laughing and Dorian was smiling and I hated them.

Talia asked questions and Dorian answered them. I didn't talk very much, except to keep Mars quiet.

"Wow, that's amazing! Do you like it?" asked Talia. "I've always wanted to go to culinary school. I can't imagine doing it in Paris. What are you making right now?"

"You're studying to be a chef?" I asked.

"Yes. At Le Cordon Bleu."

"I have to job shadow a chef," I said.

"What?" she said.

"Oh. Sorry, I'm writing this book about living in Paris and my readers challenged me to job shadow a chef for it."

"Interesting."

"Um, yeah. So could I job shadow you."

"What do you mean? You want to come to my work?"

"If that would be possible. I could just watch."

"Maybe. Let me ask my boss."

"That's so impressive," said Talia. "Do you love it?"

She paused. "No, not really. In France, cooking is kind of a blue-collar job. Plus my co-workers are really . . . hard to be around. I'm the only girl in my program. At my placement right now, I'm in a really small, hot kitchen for twelve hours a day. It's like a prison."

It seemed as if her face was made of ash.

"Are you lonely in Paris?" I blurted out. It wasn't on my list but I saw the same loneliness on her as I felt in myself.

She turned to me like she was seeing me for the first time. "Paris is a lonely place."

And then Mars cried out again and as I shushed him, she collected her things and got up to leave.

"I'm sorry. I have to be at work very early tomorrow."

"Ok well thank you so much for making time for us," said Talia. They gave bisous, kissing cheeks like the French do, but it caught me off-guard because it was our first time doing that. I guess it's easier to practice with another American. She turned to me.

"It was nice seeing you," I said. "I'll follow up about the job shadowing thing."

"Sure," she said, and pressed her face up to mine, peck peck, and I caught her scent, which smelled of vanilla and lemon.

"Bye," she said, turning to give a little wave, and then she was gone.

I HAVE ALWAYS HAD a difficult time writing about travel until after I come home. Travel resets your perceptions. Everything is so *new*! And when you don't understand the culture, the value system, it becomes impossible to know what is valuable and interesting and worth writing about, and what is not valuable, what is boring. I've done some of my best writing while I travel but I've also done my worst. On a good day, it's difficult to judge the worth of your own writing, but when you travel it becomes impossible.

You don't notice normal things—who is acting in the latest movies, the juicy gossip of the beautiful women in the table beside you, what book the man across from you is reading—you can't read the title and even if you could you wouldn't recognize the author.

Instead, you notice the color of plaster on the sides of the buildings. You notice the homeless man in the blue sleeping bag. You realize you've seen a similar blue sleeping bag, and you wonder if they're provided by the French government. You notice a crinkly plastic bag underneath a water fountain and you spend the rest of your walking thinking about it. Strange things like that, until your perceptions are raw and overwhelmed and you're not sure if you can notice anything ever again.

And this makes writing like climbing up a mountain made out of crumpled balls of tossed aside bad writing.

Writing is a redactive activity. If a picture is worth a thousand words but will be looked at only for six seconds, a story must contain a whole lifetime in a few pages. However, if you can't figure out what's interesting—certainly not the crinkling bag or the color of plaster, but what about the socialist sleeping bags?—how can you write about it? And will anyone be willing to read it?

That's why I was so excited about the next adventure, to paint Paris. While writing requires you to sift through the mess of details and select only a few important ones, painting allows you to notice and incorporate all the details.

I hoped painting would give me a way to express all the things I couldn't capture in my writing.

I also knew I was a horrible painter, and I wouldn't be able to do this adventure without help.

And so I reached out to Pauline Fraisse, a painter and writer who teaches visitors how to paint Paris. I had been following her since a little after I arrived in Paris and found her to be warm and unstuffy, even though she was a celebrated artist and taught workshops at the Louvre. We also connected because we had both travelled the world and both ran online businesses—she taught art classes and I taught writing classes—while we worked on our own artistic pursuits.

Pauline forwarded me a list of art supplies I would need,

and one afternoon I went to an art store near the Seine and bought everything. Pauline told me later it was a store Picasso liked to get his supplies from, which felt both thrilling and completely normal, since every great artist of the twentieth century had walked these streets and drunk coffee in these cafés and shopped in these shops. Everything was expensive. I spent over a hundred euro, and I thought about all the bottles of cheap amazing Rhône I could have purchased instead, and I thought about how quickly we were spending all our money in France.

Then, a few days later, I took the metro to Goncourt in the 10th arrondissement and walked the four blocks to her apartment. The 10th felt a little less gaudy than Saint Germain but also more fun, less formal. There also seemed to be a wider variety of restaurants—falafel shops, Greek restaurants, halal stands—and not the mediocre Italian and expensive-but-not-amazing French restaurants geared at tourists and wealthy locals that we had in our neighborhood.

When I got to the door to Pauline's building, I found that it was locked, needed a code. I had no service on my phone and couldn't pull up the email with the code. What could I do? I couldn't call her, obviously, with no international phone plan. Besides, I didn't know her number. So I started to hurry back the way I came, looking for a wifi signal that wasn't locked. I hustled over two blocks and found a few TMobile and other random unlocked signals, but nothing that would actually load what I needed. *Merdre.*

I was more than thirty minutes late now, and had no way to explain what had happened. Pauline and I had emailed back and forth, but we'd never met. This wasn't a good way to make a first impression.

I walked back to the building and lurked by the door,

trying to look non-threatening. After five minutes a woman with dark hair came out pushing a stroller. I held the door open for her as she maneuvered her stroller, and then snuck through the door.

Any feelings of victory were quickly dispelled. Once I got in, I was presented with a much bigger problem than the door: the labyrinthine hall was fifty feet long, had twenty apartments attached to it, and broke off into several courtyards and flights of stairs. I had Pauline's address in my email, but again, no wifi. *Merdre. Merdre. Merdre.*

It was half an hour back to my house via the metro, but I wasn't willing to give up yet. I had a foggy recollection of Pauline's address, and so I stumbled my way back through the maze of hallways to the back where I found the door I *thought* might be hers. Ever since I was a kid and stumbled into a stranger's house when I thought it was my cousin's, to be confronted by a big black lab and a strange older couple, I've been afraid of going into the wrong house. So I put my head close to the door and listened for something, the sound of Pauline's voice, hopefully. The door was soundproof, though. I couldn't hear a thing. I lingered there in the almost dark of that strange Parisian hallway, panicking for several moments before lifting my arm and rapping three times. A few moments later, the door opened and it was . . .

Pauline.

"Bonjour! Joe, right?" she said.

"Oui. Yes," I said. She leaned in to kiss cheeks and I tried not to mess it up (I was still working on my *bisous* technique).

Pauline had laid out a bottle of light white wine, a bowlful of almonds, and a few triangles of cheese. I had left my house before I could eat anything. My gut was empty. I tried not to look like a barbarian while I worked my way through her appetizers as slowly as I could.

Pauline was tall and waiflike, with fair skin, light blonde hair, and a long angular face. She spoke about how she studied at the Sorbonne in Paris and then moved to America for a year to study at Brown in Rhode Island. After school, she got a P.R. job in Paris which she didn't enjoy, and so in the early 2000s, she left France and travelled the world for a year. After her trip, she decided she didn't want to keep moving all the time but she wasn't ready to be back in France, and so she moved to Kunming, a quickly growing city in southern China. She lived there for several years and painted and taught English. She painted architecture, how the booming development led to strange juxtapositions of grubby rural old-fashioned and new firm modern. She painted walls coming up around empty farmland. She painted in watercolor and oil. She was very good.

We talked about what we would paint tomorrow. We would spend the mornings sitting in cafés sketching, or else walking around the streets of Paris, stopping from time to time to sketch the architecture, the gardens, and the people around us. And then in the afternoon we would come back to her studio to turn our sketches into paintings.

"Why sketch?" she said. "To learn how reality works."

Pauline said your sketches are your notes. It's about training your eye to see detail, shape, and perspective, to see the world as it really is and not the way our brain transforms it.

Sketching is like freewriting, like "story capture." You don't exhibit your sketches, just as you would never publish your private journals. They are resources for your own use. You sketch fast and you simplify everything, but you also look for the most important details and you sketch them as completely as you can.

But it was late now and we had to be working early at a café near Luxembourg Gardens, just a few blocks from my flat. And so I drank the last of my wine, said good night, and walked the four blocks back to Goncourt and took the metro home, and the whole way I practiced seeing how reality works, to just relax and look straight ahead and let myself be carried through the city.

EARLY THE NEXT MORNING, I arrived at Le Rostand before Pauline. I had passed this café many times but assumed it was too expensive for me. It was nice, with wood and wicker furniture on the patio and big fans and marble tabletops inside and black-and-white tiled floor and big green palms so that it felt like a garden club. I loved it, and I decided too expensive or not, I would come back another day. When Pauline arrived we sat on the patio with our sketchbooks and she told me how to draw perspective, the principles of vanishing points, and other hidden techniques artists know about the workings of reality.

I sketched an old man wearing a wide-brimmed hat and a bulky brown coat who was reading the paper. I sketched him crossing his legs and leaning back in his chair focused over the paper, and when I had finished his figure I moved on to sketch the tables around him trying to get the perspective right so that they seemed to vanish as they drew further into the patio.

As I sketched, I thought about how drawing mirrored writing. As an artist, you sketch what you see, but as a writer, you sketch the images in your imagination. You put pencil lines, structure, a bit of color into words. You capture the loose form of your story knowing you will come back later.

Sketching is like freewriting, fast and loose and simple and imperfect.

And yes, you could probably paint a masterpiece without sketching your subject beforehand, but for so many reasons, most painters don't. They prefer that extra step, that period of sketching where they can study their subject without pressure, just them, their journal, and a pencil. Sketching is free.

I hadn't finished when Pauline told me it was time to walk into the garden. We picked up our bags and sketch-books and left the cafe. We crossed Rue de Médicis and walked along the fence until we reached the entrance and then went into Jardin du Luxembourg. It was a clear, cool spring day. We sauntered to the eastern side of the fountain overlooking the palais and then sat and sketched the view of the park. I sketched the urns around the wall leading into the inner court of the park and the trees and the city behind it and the thin line of the fountain edging into the view. It was just a small sketch but it took me forty-five minutes and by the end I was exhausted with noticing things. The world was full of lines and circles and shades. I was overwhelmed with the geometry of it all.

I went back home for lunch with Talia—chicken salad sandwiches made with crème fraîche and red grapes. After a twenty-minute nap to clear my brain of the geometry, which had always been my worst subject, I took the metro back to Pauline's studio.

I painted on canvas in acrylic because oils take too long to dry (and let's be honest, because I wouldn't know what to do with them). I painted my urn and I learned that if

sketching is about capturing, painting is about inter-
pretation.

"Observe. Then make your own reality," Pauline said.

When you sketch, you try to capture the world accu-
rately, just as you would take notes in class. You want to
make sure you get everything you can down on paper. But
when you paint, you want to take that image and put as
much of yourself into it as you can fit.

I realized sketching was like a first draft and painting
was like rewriting. Rewriting was the hard part. I had
thought of freewriting as the creative part of writing, but I
realized that it was in rewriting that you put your soul into
your story.

While I tried to paint like this, I thought of Hemingway
who would walk to the Musée du Luxembourg and look at
the Cézannes and learn to write the way Cézanne painted.

"I learned how to make a landscape from Mr. Paul
Cézanne by walking through the Luxembourg Museum a
thousand times with an empty gut," he told Lillian Ross at
the New Yorker[1], "and I am pretty sure that if Mr. Paul was
around, he would like the way I make them and be happy
that I learned it from him."

I thought of Hemingway and I thought I understood
what he meant. I painted my Luxembourg urn and the way
the light traced the edges of the trees and the houses
behind it.

The next day I would walk through Paris again with
Pauline and we would go sit in the cafés of the Marais and
walk to courtyards and sketch the streetlamps and then
walk to the Place des Vosges. I would write a little too, which
was one of my adventures—"Write at the Place des Vosges,"
submitted by Arlen M.—and I would try to sketch those
famous blue rooftops but everything I would sketch that day

would feel worthless. And I would learn that painting, too, like writing, was work.

But that night in Pauline's studio I painted and was content. I painted it in flat monochrome colors and Pauline said it looked like Chirico. I was learning lessons that cannot be passed along through words. I was learning how to see the world, how to feel the world through your pencil, through your brush.

You attempt to paint your poor imitations of beauty and you learn what beauty is and how it works. You learn what color is, that it's not a word but a thousand words. You learn how to write lines into your world and how to crease back the folds of reality and paint the color happening within. You learn to write.

I finished my painting and I was content with it, even, finally, content with myself.

~

Challenge no. 5: Paint

Go to a nearby park. Either draw, write, or paint what you see. Then, share what you made in a public space (your wall, on Facebook or Instagram, or against the curb in front of your house). How do you feel about your art? How do *others* respond to it?

6

FRENCH ONION SOUP

*Eat French onion soup at Les Halles and find out why it has
become an institution. (Submitted by Winnie Q.)*

~

I t was Catherine de Medici, Catherine of the Medicis
of Florence, who first civilized France. We think of
France as this center of culture, but the truth is that
without Catherine—and Florence in general—France
would have remained the barbarian-ish conquering Gauls
they once were. It was Catherine, with her Florentine
sophistication, who brought the fork to France, Catherine
who brought her perfume-maker and introduced the
French to *eau de cologne*, Catherine who was the first to get
the French to bathe at least once a week. The history of
sophistication, at least for the last 2,000 years, flowed from
Athens to Rome to Florence and only then to Paris. And for
Paris, Catherine de Medici was the one who built the bridge.

In 1574, as her power was at its height, Catherine began
to build a new palace, an *hôtel particulier*. Perhaps she

wanted a house that would spread her taste and awe people with her power, or perhaps she wanted a home where she could grow old and die (she was fifty-five at the time, an old woman based on the life expectancy of the time), or maybe it was just what powerful people did in Europe: build a big palace so everyone will know how great you were for hundreds or even thousands of years. Legacy through construction.

Catherine's choice of location for her palace was interesting because she built a house not in the fancy section of Paris where all the important government buildings were, but in the bowels of the city, outside of the city's largest market. It might not have been that way, except for Catherine's penchant for astrology. You've heard of Nostradamus. Catherine was his main patron for many years. And so when she went to build the palace that would carry her name for the next millennium, of course she consulted her astrologers before making the decision. She had originally planned to build the home in Tuileries, right next to the Louvre and the Seine, but her astrologers? "No no," they said. "Build it there and it will crumble and your name will be lost to the wind. No, you should build it here, beside the smelly market where they sell pigs and produce instead." And she did.

Catherine de Medici built her grand palace, her Hôtel de Soissons, right next to Les Halles.

And in fewer than two hundred years it was replaced by a corn exchange. So much for legacy.

IT WAS the evening for our next adventure, and for once this was an easy one. Soup! French onion soup, which I'd eaten time and time again. Sure it was cold; sure it looked like it might rain. Welcome to early spring in Paris. No, we were going to enjoy this! I was set on it.

So with a smile on my face, I helped Talia bundle up Mars and settle him into his stroller (which I felt like I had finally come to master on the cobblestoned streets of Paris). Then we left our flat and rolled through the damp cold to the metro station. Inside it was warmer and we took the 4 line just a few stops to Les Halles.

It was sprinkling when we came up out of the metro station, and I began looking for signs. Les Halles was supposed to be this big farmer's market with stands packed together carrying the bounty of France. I had been to several farmer's markets, and Talia went to them almost every day, and had even gone on a farmer's market tour and cooking class where she learned about seasonality (buying fruits and vegetables that are in season) and how the French choose their vegetables (avoid tomatoes from Spain) and the differences between seafood in the States and Europe (European scallops still have the coral, or the ovary, which is a bright orange color and has the texture and even taste to some extent of custard). Those were the little neighborhood markets though. Les Halles was supposed to be huge, the central market of Paris for the last almost a thousand years.

Émile Zola, the great French novelist, called the market the "belly of Paris," a clever play on words since Les Halles was where you bought food but also where the poorest people in Paris would congregate. It was there you could see *real* Paris.

I had been to markets in Thailand and Vietnam and even Israel, markets that stretched for large city blocks. In Thailand everything was cheap, which meant that all the money I had been militantly opposed to spending in other, more expensive countries I found was almost instantly gone, as I spent it all on "good deals." There is something about buying a meal outside, whether seasoned chicken on a stick or crickets or noodles or onion soup, something you've never tried before, buying it from the person who made it, and then eating that meal right there, while it's still hot, wiping the juice off your chin with the back of your hand because there are no napkins. And around you the whole market is there, hundreds of people and the lights and the color and all the possibilities in the world. A meal like that can rival the best restaurants in the world. I hoped for that kind of experience at Les Halles. Perhaps it would make this trip right.

"Are you sure there's still a market here?" Talia had asked.

"What do you mean?" I said.

"I think it closed."

"I don't think so. I looked it up."

"Okay."

"I think there was a market here and they just updated it."

"Okay."

"That must be it," I said to Talia, pointing to the signs that said "Forum des Halles."

"This doesn't look right," she told me. She was right; we were in a well-groomed park with historical buildings around us and lots of concrete pathways. It didn't look like any of the markets I'd been to.

We kept walking, though, and came to a huge concrete building. A few people were going down an escalator into the building. "Forum des Halles," it said.

"I guess we should go down," I said uneasily.

"Okay."

So we went. It was a long escalator, like the ones in an

airport, and when it ended, we were in a concrete mall. No food stands, no vegetables, no meat vendors, and no onion soup.

"I guess it's not here."

"Can we find someplace with a bathroom?"

"Sure."

It was crowded now, although I'm not sure where the crowds came from, since no one was walking above us. There was an exhibit for a luxury car that people were gathering around, but the mall itself looked like something out of a third world country, cold and concrete and worn and lit with ugly halogen lights. This wasn't the market I expected. This wasn't the Paris I had been looking forward to.

We pressed through the people looking for a bathroom, but all we saw was a Starbucks. Talia went in and ordered an Americano and then used the bathroom. I waited with Mars outside the store and while I sat I connected to the internet and searched for the farmer's market.

"Les Halles de Paris, usually simply Les Halles," said Wikipedia, "was Paris's central fresh food market. Located in the heart of the city, it was demolished in 1971."

Merde.

Les Halles didn't exist anymore. And neither did its onion soup. How did this happen? Did the person who suggested this adventure really not know Les Halles *closed* more than forty years ago? How did *I* not know this?

I sat there in that cold, echoey mall outside of America's largest coffee chain and felt like all my Paris adventures were built on a lie. The Paris I had been sold was a sham. Twain wasn't in Paris; Hemingway wasn't in Paris; Baldwin wasn't in Paris; the only writers left in Paris were living off the tourism, writing books to sell outsiders an image of a city that didn't exist anymore. It was a sham. I was a sham.

What were we going to do? How was I supposed to accomplish an adventure built on a lie? How was I going to write a book about any of this? A series of adventures in the mall? I wanted to go home, drink a bottle of wine, and never think about this book again.

Talia came out of the bathroom. "You were right," I said. "This isn't the right place. Les Halles closed. Forty years ago."

She laughed.

"It's not funny," I said.

"It's a little funny."

I chuckled, I couldn't help it, and some of the tension left my shoulders.

"Okay, what do you want to do now?" she asked.

"Well, we still have to eat. Should we find some other restaurant with French onion soup?"

"Sure." We did a quick search and found a restaurant not far away that looked liked it had good onion soup and got out of that stupid mall as fast as we could.

Au Pied de Cochon, the pig's foot, was a large restaurant with red and white wicker chairs right beside where the original Les Halles had been. We got a seat outside, because even though it was cold, Mars was a culinary disaster. They turned on the outdoor heaters for us, thank God. It was pleasant sitting there at dusk, under the heaters, the park right beside us, and the round Halles aux blés, the corn exchange, with its iron dome, in our view.

We ordered our *soupe à l'oignon* and extra bread.

Julia Child was the first to introduce onion soup to the wider American culture. In France, of course, it's just called onion soup, *soupe à l'oignon*, but when Julia got a hold of it, it transformed from just plain old onion soup eaten as a side by millions to *French* onion soup, the soup enjoyed by

the   cultured,   day-time-TV-watching,   American
bourgeoisie.

For decades, until 1971 I now knew, you used to be able to
stop by Les Halles and get a bowl of soup out of a big pot for
just the loose change in your pocket. In France, onion soup
had been a meal for workers to warm up on cold afternoons,
but it was only through Julia Child, and the power of
tourism, that it became the meal of wealthy tourists lucky
enough to travel to Paris. No matter that the French eat
onion soup almost exclusively during the winter months—
December to February. Now you can order French Onion
Soup in any month at any restaurant in France, as long as it
caters to tourists.

Our soup finally came out. I balanced Mars on my knee
and brought the spoon to my mouth for the first taste.

It was . . . mediocre. The broth was too salty, the onions
cut too fine (they're supposed to be thicker, chunky, said
Talia who knows things), the cheese too sparse. The best
thing about it was that it was hot.

Why is French Onion Soup such an institution? I was
thinking about that as Mars began to lose it. I was still a new
parent and very self-conscious about making sure people
weren't disturbed by my crying child, so even though we
were outside, I picked him up, shushed him, and when he
wouldn't be shushed, took him for a walk, which quieted
him.

We walked through the park toward the great dome of
the *Bourse des commerce* (formerly the Halles aux blés, the
corn exchange). It was growing dark now, and Paris felt still
and pressed down, like you feel when you're in bed and have
a blanket over your head and nothing exists but that
moment and anything else is an interruption. I walked
around the domed building and passed a large column. I

looked up. It was tall, the tallest structure in the neighbor-hood, and beautifully designed, but what I noticed most was the bronze plaque on its side. It was the Medici Column, the last remnants of Catherine's grand palace, the one Nostradamus said was supposed to last forever. Standing there, looking at that column, I thought about the end of things, about Catherine of course but also about Les Halles and French onion soup. I thought about my book, and wondered if it was meaningless, a chasing after wind, as the teacher might say. Ecclesiastes felt appropriate in that moment. "Vanity of vanities! All is vanity." But the Hebrew word for vanity sounds like the Hebrew word for vapor. This was all vapor, wasn't it? Les Halles was vapor, Catherine's great palace was vapor, my book was vapor, even this trip was vapor. Vanity and vapor.

A chasing after wind.

You either enjoy your work and your food and drink and watch as it all disappears. Or you don't. Just don't expect to make anything that will last forever. Either way, tomorrow it will be gone.

After the trip, this book would come up in conversation and people would ask me if I'd been to France. I would get awkward, would feel like I was bragging, would feel guilty about that but also happy to have something to brag about.

"Yeah. My wife and I lived in Paris for a few months . . . in the spring," I would say.

"Wow," they would reply. "That's cool."

"Yeah, you should go. It's awesome."

But was I really awed? In that park, standing next to Catherine's ruined legacy, was I filled with wonder? Yes, it was beautiful and fascinating. But can anyone maintain wonder for months?

Paris ruins you, makes you vain, makes you drink expensive bits of coffee in tiny cups, makes you talk about your-self. Hypothesis: Perhaps I was vain before Paris. I just didn't have as much to brag about.

Is this why I went to Paris? So that people would know I had gone? Is this why I write? So that people will know I'm a writer? To what extent am I disappointed by this image I'm trying to project?

I looked up at Catherine's column. I had come to Paris to live this beautiful, adventurous life, an Instagram-worthy life. And to accomplish it, I asked for all of these challenges from my audience. And one of the challenges I got was to eat French onion soup, the most touristy food in Paris, at a marketplace that doesn't actually exist anymore and hasn't for forty years. But I kept with it, I followed through because I didn't want to disappoint, and yet it brought me to this disappointing, banal experience that was even worse because we were new parents with a baby who wouldn't sit still in the freezing weather outside a mediocre overpriced restaurant.

I was trying to live a writer's lifestyle in Paris, to go to the places Hemingway and Joyce and Fitzgerald had gone to, to soak up all the sophistication so that maybe I could use it to make something that would last forever, and yet at the very moment I was supposed to be experiencing breakthrough, I felt like a tourist. I felt like a sham. My vanity was dissolving in the wind.

When I got back Talia had already paid. The bill was thirty euro. Forty-five dollars at our exchange rate. For crappy onion soup. I started to laugh.

Why is French Onion Soup such an institution? To be honest, I still have no fucking clue.

~

Challenge no. 6: Famous Food

Is there a dish your region is famous for? French onion soup? Philly cheesesteaks? Fried chicken sandwiches? Street tacos? [1]

Go find some, then write about what it's like to eat the most clichéd food in your area. Why is *this* dish the most known food in your region? Research to find out.

7

STREET PERFORMER

Become a street performer at Notre Dame. First, you have to meet the current street performers and learn their trade. They are the main character and you are the sidekick learning from their expertise. Are they just homeless bums who beg? Or are the experts in their craft? Do they struggle to just get a few pennies or do they make serious bank off their entertainment? Why do they do it?

Overcome your "writer self" and put yourself out there to perform . . . be watched, be criticized, be viewed by people who don't know who you really are and are just judging their perception of you.
(via Laura J.)

I hadn't spoken to Bethany since she had dropped us off at the airport, but a few weeks into our trip she texted that she had a long layover in Paris and should she come visit us?

"Of course!" we told her.

And a few weeks after that, she did visit. Talia, Mars, and I waited for her at the Saint Germain metro stop. When she came up the steps, her face was glowing, all lit up by Paris, seeing it for the first time.

Talia hugged her. I hugged her. She tickled Mars' toes.

"Mars, you've gotten so big," she squealed.

Was that true? We had been gone for more than a month. Had he changed so much? I kept thinking about this as we walked. Talia was showing off all the things in our neighborhood, and I watched Bethany ooh and ah over everything I now took as normal.

How quickly we stop seeing, I thought. *How quickly we lose our wonder. Just as we don't notice our child growing up before our eyes, we lose the ability to be captured by the most beautiful city in the world. Noticing is a discipline*, I thought, and I was grateful our friend could teach us again to see.

I carried Bethany's bags up the stairs to our apartment, unlocked the door, and set them down in the living room.

"Wow. These beams are amazing," she said. "And your kitchen is so tiny and perfect. Is this a Nespresso machine? How awesome! Let me look out the window? Oh my God that's amazing."

"You must be starving," said Talia.

I followed them back out of our apartment and we walked to Rue de Buci where we sat for a late lunch at a streetside cafe. Talia ordered steak frites and I got Bethany to order a croque monsieur, because it's the quintessential French café sandwich, made with ham and cheese between two slices of brioche with more cheese baked over the top. We didn't have much money and so I didn't order anything and instead had bites of each and it was all delicious but that might have been because I was so hungry.

I took Bethany on "the walk" to all our favorite places,

starting from our apartment to the Luxembourg gardens where they ordered *chocolat* at Angelina's (I had sips) and then around the loop through the gardens with the palace in the center. We left the gardens to walk up to Gérard Mulot for a baguette and then up to the Seine and across Pont des Arts and to the glass pyramids in the courtyard of the Louvre. There is a window through one of the arches there where you can see into a room full of sculptures without paying to get inside or waiting in the horrible line, and so we sat there at a bench for a while eating bread and looking at the sculptures.

"This is so good." Bethany tore off another chunk of baguette—we all did—and when the baguette was gone we left the Louvre and walked along the quai and across Pont d'Arcole to Île de la Cité and then there was Notre Dame.

I had been to Notre Dame many times by then, of course, but seeing it through someone else's eyes I was awed again.[1] It seemed in motion, rising up out of that tiny island with its insectile flying-buttress-legs. But it was also imperiously still and quiet. The pigeons roosted in the crevices and faces of saints watched us in silence.

Bethany and Talia went in to do a free lap around its chapels—not the climb to the tower, which costs money—but I stayed outside and watched the crowds and the street performers, thinking perhaps I would find someone to shadow for my challenge.

There was a five-piece dixie jazz band playing on one of the bridges, complete with a piano and an upright bass—I have no idea how they got the piano there. I had seen them before, because they often played on Boulevard Saint Germain across the street from Les Deux Magots, and so I felt possessive of them, like they shouldn't be over here, they should be back by our house where they belonged.

But I didn't want to shadow the jazz band.

There was a golden man in a top hat. His entire body was painted, his face and hands and clothes. Only the whites of his eyes weren't gold. He didn't move. You couldn't even tell he blinked unless you watched him for a long time. It was only when someone put money in his hat, and even then not every time, that he would do a stiff little motion, a wave or a bow.

But I didn't want to shadow the golden man.

Then I heard a speaker playing music and I saw a circle forming. I walked over to take a look and that's when I first saw the man with the soccer ball.

He wore gym clothes and a backwards hat and he tapped the ball up into the air and then caught it on the top of his foot and held it perfectly still, then *pop* it was up in the air and now on his nose, and then he knocked it back in the air and he was bowing forward and the ball fell on his back and would have fallen to the ground but then he pulled up his shirt and caught it behind his back; the ball still in his shirt, he hoola-hooped it around his waist and then punched it back where it came from. The ball dropped out of his shirt to fall on his feet again and in a single motion it was up and then he caught it again on his foot but then held it with his ankle and he leapt forward into a handstand, the ball still clutched between his foot and his shin. He posed like that standing on his hands with his legs splayed out and the ball clinging to his foot for several seconds.

Which is to say he was amazing.

This is the guy, I thought. *I need to shadow HIM.*

But then he was packing up to leave. I knew I should go up and talk to him. This was my chance. But I was rooted to the spot. He was winding up the cable from his speaker and then gathering up the hat full of money, but still I didn't say anything to him. I didn't, *couldn't*, move. I turned to see Talia and Bethany coming out of Notre Dame and when I looked back he was gone.

We walked home by the Seine. Talia pointed out Shake-speare and Co. bookstore to Bethany and they talked about the Latin quarter, but I was quiet. I had missed my chance. I felt so stupid. I had waited too long, as usual. My fear of talking to strangers had paralyzed me and the one chance I had since I arrived in Paris to find a street performer had slipped right past me like a bright-painted boat floating in the Seine.

What's wrong with you?

"What did you say, Joe?"

"Oh sorry. I was just talking to myself."

The days went by and I kept searching for street performers, mostly without luck. One day I saw a big brass band marching through the streets in Montmartre, but I ignored the thought to go talk to them. We got halfway down the hill, and I changed my mind.

"I'll be right back." I handed Mars' stroller to Talia.

"Where are you going?" Talia shouted after me.

But when I got there they were already dispersed, hopped away with their instruments like a basketful of crickets.

Another day I was with Talia having a glass of wine at a café when I heard the sound of hand drums. They were echoing through the streets and getting closer. Then I saw a group of men come around the corner. They weren't wearing shirts and their bare chests shone with sweat, dancing to the drums. The group reached a spot in the middle of the street near our table. The drums kept playing. Then one of the men broke off from the group, backflipped into the air then crouched down in the street. Another broke off and came after him. The second threw a hard punch across the body of the first who dodged away and twisted into a roundhouse kick. I was drinking a glass of Rhône in France while watching a street fight. It was the strangest thing. They kept up like that, punching, dodging, roundhouse kicking, ducking. I watched. Everyone watched.

"I should go talk to them," but even as I said it, the anxiety echoed in my gut.

By then they were already down the street and two new performers were squaring off from each other as the drummers of the group played on.

Trying to ignore the fear in my gut, I got up from the table and jogged after them. I went up to a big guy, maybe 6' 3", at the edge of the group. He smiled and I smiled and I asked, "Parlez-vous anglais?" And he nodded.

"Are you street performers?" I asked.

"Yes." He handed me a flier. "We are performing for our gym." I tried to read the flier but it was in French, something about jiu-jitsu classes. They were street performers advertising a gym, then. Interesting.

"Can anyone join?"

"Yes."

"Do you perform like this very often?"

"No."

"Oh."

I thanked him and waved and walked back to my table. *Nice, Joe. You finally work up the courage to talk to a street performer and you pick the one who can't help you. Real great.* I got back to the table and ordered another glass of wine.

I BEGAN to research the street performance scene online, and the more I learned, the harder I realized this was going to be, and it was all for one reason: French bureaucracy. I found out that if you want to be a street performer in Paris, whether you're a golden man mime or a dixie band with a grand piano, you have to have a permit. And to get a permit you have to go in front of a bunch of judges which meets once every six months or so and show your stuff. And if, for instance, someone actually DID let me perform with them and we were caught, they could lose their permit, which meant no good street performer would want me to perform with them.

How was this going to work? It was bad enough I had to overcome my own breed of social anxiety; I also had to over-come French bureaucracy? Ughghghghhghghghghgh. Remind me why I signed up for this?

But as I was researching I stumbled on a government website with a picture of a guy juggling a soccer ball. I clicked through a few links and found myself reading about a young Parisian street performer who had played soccer on a semi-pro team for a few years and then switched from playing games to juggling a soccer ball in front of places like SacréCœur, Notre Dame, and the Trocadéro.

I looked at the photo. Was it him? Could it be?

It could. It was.

Iya Traoré was the guy with the soccer ball in front of Notre Dame.

Even better, he had a website with a contact form. Talking to strangers on the street might freak me out, but I could *email* anyone. Even so, I had a few butterflies in my stomach as I typed out my note to Iya.

"BONJOUR MONSIEUR IYA," I wrote. "I'm a writer and jour-nalist and am working on a book based in Paris. I've read about you and seen some of your skills online. I believe I even saw you performing in Paris. I would like to watch your performance and interview you for my book. Would you be willing to do that? Please let me know if you're interested! Sincerely, Joe."

He probably wouldn't respond, but then I now knew where to track him down. This was the best chance I had to complete my challenge. It might not work out, but if it did it would be amazing.

I checked my email later that night and nearly dropped my phone when I saw a response from Iya.

"I am interested for your regquest if you can paye me," it said. (I've left the spelling errors in there for effect.)

I didn't mind Iya asking for money. When you're a street performer, I imagined, you have to hustle to make it work. I didn't even mind that his email bore a lot of resemblance to the email I also received that day about my inheritance from the crowned prince of Nigeria. I thought I would probably spell "request" and "pay" wrong too if English was my third language after French and my native tongue. Still, it was something of a red flag. Looking back, there are all the signs of the disaster that was to come.

"I'm fairly sure I can do that," I kept pressing. "What would make a really great story, Iya, is if you taught me some of your skills. Perhaps, I could try to perform what you do in front of an audience, and then you could show off how much better you are. I'd be happy to pay for this and the interview. What would be a fair price for your time? Best, Joe."

Iya, or his agent, responded the next afternoon:

· · ·

WE RECEIVED your request with Iya.

I am interested for your regquest if you can paye me 1000euro

The traveling costs, the food, or the hotel if need are chargeable to the customer.

As a result of a huge number of requests, we would be grateful if you could reply to us shortly in order to make sure that Iya will be available for your event.

Best regards, and have a nice day

PS: please find attached Iya's show press book

INCLUDED WAS a thirty page PDF showing Iya appearing on both local and international television shows, in newspapers, and in magazines, plus some bonus photography that was watermarked. He—or his agent—also linked to three videos on YouTube. They were conveniently labeled: Iya Traoré Best of 2 minutes, Iya Traoré History 5minutes, and Performance live TV.

I clicked on the link to Iya Traoré Best of 2 minutes. If I thought watching him in front of Notre Dame was amazing, the video was even more so. It showed him on the French equivalent to X Factor, spinning a soccer ball on a straw balanced on his mouth; it showed juggling on the wall in front of SacréCœur at sunset with two drummers keeping the beat; it showed him climbing the lampposts on Sacré-Cœur shirtless, his eight-pack abs glistening in the sunset, all of Paris behind him.

But I did not have one thousand euro. I didn't even have the ten to go up to the top of Notre Dame. I emailed him:

THANKS FOR YOUR RESPONSE IYA. I'm definitely interested in

getting to know you and I'm happy to provide an honorarium. You're certainly worth 1,000€. I only wish I could afford it. I wish you all the best and good luck in your career, Iya.

Joe

IYA HAD GREATER hopes for me than I had for him, though. He emailed me just a few hours later:

HOW MUCH U can paye me?

I APPRECIATED THAT HE RESPONDED, and especially the fact that he was consistent in his spelling of "regquest." Is that how the French spelled it?

How much can I pay you? Good question, Iya, I thought as I sipped from my cold thimble of coffee in a café I couldn't afford. I did have some money still set aside for challenges, but as I checked my account I saw how quickly it was dwindling. The mistakes you make for art.

I thought about paying it. Should I just give him the thousand euro? I sort of had the money. Was this the one thing I wanted to spend it on? Was this one adventure worth a thousand euro? I wished I had enough money to solve all my problems. But even if I did, I knew that it wouldn't work. Would money alone have made it easier to talk to Iya in front of Notre Dame?

I wallowed for a while in Coutume. I played Sudoku. But then the thought occurred to me, what would Laura J. do? She was the one who challenged me to do this. How would she handle this situation?

And then I remembered I wasn't alone on this. I had a

whole community of people with me, a team of problem solvers (and maybe counselors). My audience had felt like a burden for most of this trip, like a few tens of thousands of people I had to carry on my back through Paris. I knew I signed up for it, but that didn't always make it easier. But now I realized they were also a resource.

So I posted a summary of the conversation with Iya online and asked my audience how they would handle it.

While I waited for their responses to come through, I left my café and rented a Vélib and then pedaled through the streets of Paris. I didn't know where I was going until I found myself in front of Notre Dame. It was a cool weekday morning and the square around the cathedral was all but empty. There were no street performers, and I found it to be a relief. I sat on a bench and watched the birds land on the gargoyles and the few tourists walk through the square and take selfies and then turn into the cathedral.

I thought back to the days when I actually would have leapt at a challenge like this, when I used to play guitar on the streets of Santa Barbara, a twenty-three-year-old aspiring songwriter who dreamed of being up on stage and wanted to perform for thousands of people. And yet every time I would go to perform it made me want to throw up and then find a dark corner to hide in and take a nap. The cold and the guitar strings would bite into my fingers and people would walk past never making eye contact just looking at my open guitar case, with the few rumpled bills that were almost all mine. I remember playing one Friday night for the people going to the clubs and a drunk guy gave me a ten-dollar bill. It had been the only money I'd made that night, and I think he thought it was a dollar. I had left early, exhausted and unsatisfied. Proud too. I had done it, gotten through it, survived. There was a rush to performing, but it left me feeling wrung out.

I quit trying to be a songwriter not long after that. I focused on writing articles and books because then you didn't have to feel like you were going to throw up. Sure you still felt like you wanted to hide sometimes, but you also *could* hide behind a computer screen in a warm café somewhere. You didn't have to be out in the open for everyone to see.

And yet here I was again, the same old fears. What was I going to do?

I got back on my Vélib and pedaled home. As I rode my phone chimed with a calendar notification and when I got to a stoplight I pulled it out to check. It was a reminder for the slam poetry meetup I had been invited to read at later that day. The founder was an English poet and novelist who had moved to Paris and created the group for expat writers to perform their work. I had some interest in seeing the local writing scene, but I had no plans to perform. Let the extroverts do that, I thought, the people who actually like this stuff.

When I got home I found my idea to ask my audience for help had paid off. I had a half-dozen suggestions for my adventure. One person said I should just go stand on a bench with a hat out and dance. Someone else told me to just abandon the adventure entirely and pick a different one. Another asked, "Do you have to perform in front of Notre Dame? Couldn't you find somewhere else to perform something, maybe karaoke or something?"

I laughed it off at first, but then something occurred to me.

Does it have to be Notre Dame?

I needed to "overcome my writer self," but could I do that somewhere else?

Somewhere else. Where else? I was doing a search on karaoke bars near us when I remembered the poetry group.

How do I best overcome my introverted writer self? How could I put myself out there to perform and be watched and criticized?

What better way than by performing *my writing*? I had already been talking to the people at the poetry group. If not Notre Dame, what better place to perform, to *shadow* a performer than a slam poetry meetup?

I knew what I had to do. I was a little terrified about it, but I was also excited.

MY METRO MAP was fading to white along the edges where I had creased it and put it in my pocket dozens of times. I needed it less often now, but I still kept it there in my pocket for moments when I was going somewhere new, moments like tonight. I was on the II line, which I always enjoyed, even though it took a little longer, because there was this one station, Arts et Métiers, that looked like the inside of the submarine from *Twenty Thousand Leagues Under the Seas*. The walls were covered in copper panels riveted together, and every dozen paces were portholes with zeppelins and spaceships and cathedrals and gears behind the glass, all in a chipper steampunk style. It cheered me up to go through and reminded me that this was Paris and not New York or London or Chicago or some other big city's metro. Sometimes underground you felt it was all the same.

I was anxious, which meant I was sleepy. I always get sleepy when I have anxiety. I don't know why; maybe my body's overcorrecting attempt to calm itself down. I felt my back, my shoulders, so taut it felt like the seams were ripping out. The movement of the train was giving me nausea.

I must be performing tonight, I thought. *Nothing makes me feel as terrible as performing.*

I left the metro at Goncourt and then walked grumpily the few blocks to Au Chat Noir, a bar in the 11ᵗʰ arrondissement (named after Le Chat Noir, the seventeenth century Montmartre cabaret beloved by Picasso and other bohemians). It was warm inside and packed. A motley assortment of American, British, Italian, and French, all of them writers. They were supposed to be my kind of people but I hated them all. I ordered a beer—just three euro, which felt like nothing compared to six-fifty at Café de la Mairie—and I sipped self-consciously while glancing around at all the people and trying to decide whether I really wanted to talk to anyone. I didn't want to, of course. But I knew I had to, if only to get my name on the list.

A nerdy guy with curly hair and a worn black sportcoat stood at the bar beside me. He had a nervous twitchy way of moving, and I thought, *now here is someone more awkward than me, if that's possible*. We made eye contact then and while I looked away at first I looked back and then smiled a tight lipped smile. I knew I should introduce myself but I felt that same paralysis come over me that I had felt in front of Notre Dame. I felt it reaching down my throat and into my gut trying to drown me. *Should I say something*, I asked myself, *when it's this hard?* Yes, I heard. *Should I really try to fight this when I could just say nothing and it would be so much easier?* Yes, I should. Merdre.

"Hi. I'm Joe." I turned to the curly-haired man.

"I'm sorry?" he said, shouting. I didn't realize how loud it was.

"I'm Joe." I stuck my hand out.

"It is. Nice to meet you Joe."

"Are you a writer?" I stepped closer so I didn't have to shout as loud.

"I am. I write poetry. I have a series of poems about pigeons. Pigeons in Paris. I write about what they're thinking and their perspective of the city and what I'm thinking about as I wonder what they're thinking about. I'm turning them into a book right now."

Well. Definitely someone more awkward than me here.

I talked to David for several minutes and then he left to talk to his wife who was also a writer in the group.

Then I recognized Albert from the group's website. He helped run the group and while I thought about not doing it, the conversation with David had given me a little momentum and so I walked up to him.

"Hey, are you Albert?"

"I am." He smiled.

I told him I was working on a book about Paris and asked him a couple of questions about the group.

"Did you sign up to do a reading yet?" His voice reminded me of someone. I couldn't put my finger on it.

"I haven't yet, no."

"Are you going to? I have the list right here. There are only a few spots and they go quickly."

"Um . . ." This was it. My last chance to back out. I had a sudden desire to throw down my coat and fall asleep in the corner of the bar. "Yes. Sign me up for the second round."

He wrote my name down. Well. There was no turning back now. I really needed a nap.

SOMEONE RANG a loud handbell and people began filtering

through the bar down the stairs to the basement where row after row of benches were set up around a small clearing in the center of the room, the place the poet would stand. The place I would stand not too long from now.

Albert was in the center. He was wearing a top hat and smiling. A man with hair to his shoulders sat at a piano in the corner and played a vaudeville jingle and Albert lifted his arms to welcome everyone in. The air was hot and I felt like this whole thing was bohemian and grungy but also amazingly well put together, and if I wasn't performing I would have been so glad to be there.

"WELCOME everyone to Slam Poetry in Paris," said Albert in a sing song circus voice, "our WEEKLY meetup for POETS and MISFITS." I realized I knew exactly what his voice reminded me of and started laughing to myself. It was Gru from the Disney film Despicable Me, the main character with the Romanian accent, and even though Albert was Italian he sounded exactly the same.

"Our FIRST poet of the night is Frank Jones reading a poem. Everyone say a CHAT NOIR bonjour to FRANK!"

Frank was a wide-set balding man with a fedora and a New York accent. He came up to the stage like someone who'd been on one all his life and introduced his poem, which was about jazz, which he said he played professionally, and New York. David stood by the door and when Frank began he pulled the door shut because apparently there was no lock and he was the one designated to keep the door shut so no one would be distracted during the reading. Frank was a good poet and it made you feel cool and sophisticated like smoking French cigarettes (I imagined), and when he finished a few people clapped but everyone else snapped, which did feel like the right thing to do.

Then the vaudeville piano was going and Albert came back on stage.

"Tonight's FEATURED poET comes all the way from PRAGUE where she's a poet in RESidence. PLEASE give a WARM welcome to Dana Toulon!"

A pretty, thin young woman came to the stage and launched into her first poem, a long piece addressed to a brief boyfriend she had in Paris. She had an English accent and read about walking the streets late at night drunk and making love on the Champs-Élysées (I'll always remember how she pronounced it, "llllllluuuv," just rolling on the l forever). I thought for a long time about the practicalities of sex on the most touristed street in the world. It sounded uncomfortable at the very least. Poets, man. She finished and people clapped. I think everyone was still a bit confused about that sex part. But then the piano snapped us out of it and Albert was leaping back up to the front.

"Our LAST performer for THIS act is our very own DAVID!" The room erupted for my pigeon poet friend. He walked, twitchy and smiling, up to the stage, unfolding a poem from his shirt pocket.

"This is a poem I wrote about a pigeon," he said, and everyone cheered again.

He read his first poem and it was amazing, short and funny and perfectly clear. Everyone laughed at the funny parts and then felt reflective and awake at the end, and when he finished and they cheered again I found that I had tears in my eyes, I was so happy.

The first break came. I went upstairs and paced around. I didn't feel sick now that I was there. I felt excited and nervous and exhausted. I thought, *wouldn't it be nice to not have to do this, to just enjoy the poetry and the stories. Wouldn't it be great to just observe, to be a fan. Why go through the trouble of performing? It will just ruin it anyway.* I didn't talk to anyone. After a few minutes I went back downstairs and took out the paper I had brought with me.

There were just a few people down in the basement. A group of students sat talking nearby. I felt exposed to be down there alone, talking to no one, just looking nervously down to my notes. But how could I go upstairs and when it felt like my muscles were going to burn up every moment?

It felt like a long time before they rang the bell and people began coming downstairs. When they all sat down I noticed the room was half as full as it was during the first session, and I felt let down, like I was going through all of this and no one cared.

We went through four poets and one songwriter. I thought they were all just okay, but I'm always a harsh critic before I perform. And then Albert was calling me.

"And next we have Joe Bunting, who is reading a piece of fiction."

I have no recollection of getting up and making my way to the front. The pianist may have played filler music while I went up. I don't remember. I'm sure I looked up when I got to the front and smiled as well as I could and said hello. I'm sure I introduced my story, explained the context of the excerpt, and began reading. But I have no recollection of that. I only remember waking up a few seconds into the story and realizing, hey, here I am. I'm reading this. I'm performing!

I remember the dry feeling in my mouth.

I remembered to fix my posture and lift my creaking back.

I remember trying not to trip over my words, and when I did, praying that it was the last time.

I remember reading, "There are limits to everything,

even genius. And soon all of life is chained up empty space."
I remember both feeling like it was profound in that
moment but also wondering if they would really get it.

I remember tears coming to my eyes.

I remember ignoring them.

But I don't remember finishing my reading, saying thank
you. I don't remember the applause, except that I believe I
felt like I should have been getting more for how hard it had
been to get up there. I don't remember a single other poet or
performer after that; well, except Albert, who took off the
top hat to read a poem about traveling in Spain.

Then it was over. I was upstairs with Albert and a prim
Parisian guy, drinking cheap beers and celebrating our
performances.

"Your story was very good," Albert told me. "Sometimes
when people read stories you can't follow it and you start to
fall asleep. But I followed your story the whole time."

"Thank you," I said. "I loved your poem. It felt a little
like Byron."

The prim Parisian guy was about my age. He said he was
from Paris but spoke English with an Australian accent. I
could tell he came from money because he said all he did
was write even though he had only published one book that
hadn't sold very well. He was very kind though. He told me
about the fashion parties and midnight raves he went to and
I thought this was a Paris I would probably never see and
was happy it existed and sad I would never be part of it.

They asked me about my book and I told them and they
acted impressed when I told them about the adventures I
had done and the audience I had online who was cheering
me on. When I mentioned the catacombs Albert perked up.

"So you have not BEEN to the ilLEGAL and unSANC-
TIONED parts yet?"

"I haven't! I need to but this cataphile keeps putting me off. He keeps saying he's moving when I ask him to meet and tells me to try later."

"I have the guy you need to talk to."

"Who is it?"

"His name is Gilles."

"Wait. Gilles?"

"Yes, Gilles. He's my friend."

"I know exactly who that is."

And I did. Because when I had prepared for my first adventure, I had read everything I could find about the catacombs. There were articles in National Geographic, the New York Times, the Wall Street Journal, and on National Public Radio. Gilles was in *all* of them. In many ways, he was the most famous cataphile in the world.

And then Albert slid a piece of paper with his email address across the table.

Challenge no. 7: Perform

Get four friends and five umbrellas and go with you to a public area like a mall, shopping center, monument, or street corner (if you don't *have* four friends, you have to *make* them)! Then perform a flash mob dance, choreographed to the song "Singing in the Rain."

Take a video and post it to social media with the hashtag #crowdsourceadventure.

8

CHEF

Job shadow a chef in Paris. (From Kristen P. and Kacie A.)

T he metro was closed by the time I left Au Chat Noir and then I got spectacularly lost on the bike ride home. When I finally made it back to Saint Germain at nearly three in the morning, I walked quickly up the last stairs to my apartment. I put the key in and turned the lock and was expecting darkness when I opened the door.

But instead the light was on. Talia was glaring at me, red-eyed.

"Where the hell have you been?" she said.

It took a few seconds to catch my breath and figure out what was going on.

I laughed. I shouldn't have. It was the worst thing to do. But I couldn't help it. I couldn't transition from the adventure I had just been part of, to this, an angry wife and a disheveled flat.

Her reply was a withering stare that felt like a bucket of the Seine poured over my head.

"I missed the metro and had to ride a bike back," I said. "And then I got a little lost."

"I was about to call the police," she said. "I was about to wake Mars up and go out and search the streets for your body."

Most of Talia's brown hair was pulled back in a limp ponytail but there were big clumps escaping on the sides of her face. She was in red plaid pajamas and a big bathrobe and had a crazed look on her face.

"I didn't know that," I said. I put my stuff down on the table, my phone, my briefcase which held all my writing, my wallet, and my keys to the apartment. I usually would have put most of these things on the table beside the bed (i.e. the fold-out couch that was serving as our bed), but that would have meant climbing over the bed with a very enraged Talia in it and I wasn't ready to risk getting that close to her just yet.

"Is that all you have to say?"

"I don't know what you want me to say. I just rode all over Paris and got lost like six times. I'm sorry you've been worried and stressed this entire time. I didn't meant to do that and I tried to get home sooner. I would have called but we didn't get cell phone plans with service because we had no money." I also didn't say *and also had one of the best nights and best adventures since arriving in Paris*, but maybe she saw it on my face because she was not impressed.

"You could have texted."

"My phone was out of battery!"

"I don't know then. Find a bar with a phone, Joe, but when you're out until three in the morning, I don't know what you expect! God, I've been trying to explain this to you for months but you just don't listen!"

"What have you been trying to explain for months?"

"That you have to communicate, JOE! That it's not ok to just do your own thing and expect your family to work around you. You've been in your head this whole trip, doing these adventures that no one else in your family signed up for . . ."

"I ASKED you if I should write this book and you said YES," I said.

"YES the book! But then it became this huge thing and we never talked about it."

"So what? You want me to quit now?"

"NO, but we've never even talked about it, JOE. You're never focused on me. You never tell even tell me you love me."

"I tell you ALL the time."

"Not without me telling you first."

"That's not fair. You know I love you."

"Do I? You're more focused on France and your adventures than me. I've been trying to tell you this for months. YEARS really and you don't listen. I can't do this anymore."

"What do you mean you can't do this anymore?"

"You need to talk to someone else about this. I can't keep explaining it."

I sat there trying to think of something to say, the pause stretching out. I thought of other things. I looked at the cabinets on the walls. I thought about how little I wanted to be here in this moment. I thought of the other things I could be doing. The episode of TV I could be watching to wind down from my ride. The games of Sudoku I could be playing. The shower I could be having. The sleep I could be getting.

I realized that nothing had changed.

All I wanted was to move to Paris and escape my boring small-town life, my dull routine, my moments of being a bad husband, my uninspiring existence. I thought Paris would solve all my problems, but it didn't. I still had all the same problems plus a few new ones too.

I was trying to escape my prison and I brought it with me.

You can't flee your prisons. You can't impress people out of them; you can't Instagram your way out. The prison is you. We are our prisons. Loving other people isn't enough. How can we be free until we know ourselves, love ourselves?

If I ever want to be a real writer, I realized, *I need to look at life in the face. If the prison is me, I need to embrace it, to stop fleeing it, to turn the prison into a garden full of life, a place that can offer life and joy and happiness and peace to the world.*

Talia checked her phone, which had just buzzed.

"Are you seriously going to do that right now?" I said.

"Oh my God."

Her jaw fell.

"Dorian just tried to kill herself. She's in the hospital."

HÔPITAL DE LA PITIÉ-SALPÊTRIÈRE was in the 13th arrondissement, southeast of our apartment near the very edge of Old Paris. Google ominously labels it a "teaching hospital with a turbulent history" because it was originally a gunpowder factory in the 1700s, and then a kind of dumping ground for sex workers and the poor in Paris. Louis XIV eventually converted it into a hospital—not just a jail for prostitutes—but even then it specialized in treating the mentally ill.

When the French Revolution broke out, a mob broke into Salpêtrière to free the 134 sex workers who were imprisoned there, a noble thing, but they also led out the twenty-five women who were considered insane—probably for disagreeing with their husbands or failing to obey their fathers—and murdered them in the streets. Less noble.

The hospital was partly responsible for modern psychology, since it was here that Sigmeund Freud studied with Jean-Martin Charcot, the pioneer of neurology. Freud would later say it was his time at Salpêtrière that led him to consider studying psychopathology.

It was the afternoon after we first got word about Dorian, and I was still exhausted and bleary eyed from the previous night's adventure (as was Talia, I'm sure, though she was too proud to say), but still Mars and I took the metro to the 13th and walked the few blocks into a confusing campus of mid-rise buildings whose architecture was half ornately-Romantic and half 1960s-modern. All ugly, in other words.

The hospital was very confusing to navigate, and alone I would have had no idea where to find Dorian's room. The buildings weren't labeled well and the signs were all in French anyway.

But fortunately Talia had been there the night before, and she said, "I think this is the right one," as we walked into another twenty-story, ugly concrete building.

"This is where they wheeled her in," she said. But it was just a hall with a service elevator and doctors and techs scurrying through to the next place.

"Are you sure we can get up this way?" I asked.

"No."

"Should we keep looking?"

"Sure." Talia turned around and we went back outside. But when we asked someone for directions, they pointed us back into the room we had just left. That's when we saw the regular elevator and went up.

Hospitals in every country look the same: bland decor, confusing hallways, busy people scurrying through. Salpêtrière was no different. At the same time, the language difference made it feel, to me, more inhospitable. I already felt like I was always trespassing in hospitals. Here I felt out of place even breathing in one.

When we got to Dorian's section, no one else was there. The nurse spoke English, and told us two people were allowed to go back at a time, but that Mars would have to stay out of the room.

"I'll go. But can you get us food?" she asked. "I'm starving."

I was honestly relieved. I wanted to support Dorian. I wanted to ask her all my questions, and to tell her she looked like ash when we saw her before, and that I knew what loneliness was and that hers didn't scare me, she could be free around us, but the idea of being alone with her also made me anxious.

"Sure. I'll go get something."

It took me an hour, but I found a grocery store just across from the hospital and splurged on sandwiches for everyone, plus some soup for Dorian, thinking she might not be enjoying the hospital food. I waited with Mars in a bright corridor. He ate bread and bites of an apple and pieces of tomato from my sandwich. He ate in his stroller until he whined and then on my lap and then the floor and the seat beside me and anywhere else he felt like while I tried to keep him entertained, and he left a stream of crumbs and sticky apple skins along the antiseptic hospital floor.

Then Joy came out of the elevator and into the corridor. She was tall and had strawberry-blonde hair pulled into a bun and a huge smile on her face, as she always did. It felt like life had just came back into the building and into our lives.

"HEY Joe!" she said, hugging me.

"When did you get in?" I asked.

"I just got off the plane and caught the metro here."

"Wow. How was the trip?" I asked.

"It was great. Dude, thank you SO much for being here. I told Talia already but it's so amazing that you guys were here and able to take care of Dorr."

"Of course, Joy." I didn't say then how lonely we were, that even this bit of contact in between nurse visits and open hours with Dorian had been a gift, that even standing there with her for that moment was like water on a hot day.

Joy went in, but I stayed outside with Mars and walked him in the stroller in a slow rectangle, twelve paces along the corridor, two paces across the hall, twelve paces back, two paces across, twelve, two, twelve, two, until Mars slept but I still paced like that for a long time, afraid he would wake.

I had wanted a new walk back in that small town. I had left everything for a new walk, a new beautiful Parisian walk, and here I had found it and it was smaller and less exciting than I could have ever imagined it, and yet for the first time I was happy, content, because at last—AT LAST!— we were being real. I had wanted more Instagram followers and to make people envious, but really I should have settled for being more real, more raw, more open, more myself. I may still have left that small town, but I might have also saved myself and my family a lot of disappointment along the way if I had realized that earlier.

And just then they pushed a hospital bed through the door and it was Dorian.

I stopped pacing.

Her face was yellow. She saw me and she smiled at me, the smallest smile in the world, and waved.

I told someone once if you want to be a writer you can never look away. You have to be willing to stare at it all in the face, at death and vanity and hopelessness and suicide, all if it in the face, to truly see it for what it is. Only then can you write the truth. I realized I had been looking away for too long, for months, for years, maybe. Talia had tried to tell me and I had been missing it. Seeing Dorian, I realized I needed to do better; she deserved better from me.

I smiled back. I wished I could have done more, but I couldn't think of anything more in that moment, but in my smile I tried to let encouragement and hope come through, but who knows whether smiles can transmit such things. I felt like I wasn't enough. I never was enough. And then she was gone and a few minutes later Talia came out.

"Ready to go?" she said.

"Sure. Is Joy going to stay?"

"Yeah."

"Okay."

We walked back to the metro and took the train back to Saint Germain, and not for the first time in Paris, I felt tired down to my bones.

JOY MET us for drinks later that afternoon at Café de la Mairie after dropping Dorian at a session with her assigned therapist. It was a beautiful spring day. We sat outside and the canopies that were a fixture during the cold days were all down and I pieced together what had really been going on.

Dorian was in a relationship with a guy from her culinary school. He wasn't from Paris either, was Singaporean, and apparently made the best croissants in his entire school —the secret was to let the butter rest a moment in between folds, he would tell me later. But things weren't going well between him and Dorian. He liked her, had even said he loved her, but Dorian had wanted him to be something more, or something different anyway—more interesting, more charming, more focused on her, more in love.

"I don't think I'll ever be who you want me to be," he had told her.

It didn't end as much as get awkward. They stopped spending much time together, and when they did, they would either fight or she would pretend it was fine, they could still be friends. And really, who else did she have to be friends with? And then she found she was wondering what it felt like to die, and one thing led to another and soon she was washing down a bottle of painkillers with a bottle of wine and then freaking out and calling the boyfriend who broke into her apartment and then called the ambulance. I don't know if I would have done the same, but I understood it.

I don't remember what we talked about after that but I remember laughing for the first time in months. Joy was there. We had a friend! This is what we had dreamed Paris would be. I drank white wine because it was a euro cheaper but picked up the bill when it came and wouldn't let Joy pay. "You can get the next one," said Talia.

"Yeah, next time we're going to Spring," I said.

Then Joy was gone, back to the hospital.

I lay in bed late that night and remembered the tea shop where we'd first met. I remembered Dorian talking so quietly, and when she talked about Paris it was with a dryness that I'd never seen from anyone who lived in that city. There are a lot of expats who end up not liking Paris, and I understand that, but when Dorian started talking about her life there it was like she was breathing ash and her face was ash and her mouth and her guts were ash too.

I began to get angry. Why didn't Dorian tell us that she had a boyfriend when we first met her? They were still together then. She had her boyfriend and he was in her class but she never told us. And when she came to a dinner party we'd had at our house she didn't ask us if she could bring her boyfriend or anyone else. She showed up an hour late and she didn't bring anything and just lied to us all night long, lied to us ever since we had met her.

I got angry first, and then got sad, sad because I felt what Dorian had felt and knew I understood it, not the depths of it but the beginnings of it and had been there too, at the beginnings not the depths. I felt sad because I should have done more.

But then I began to feel kind of okay and then kind of excited, which I know is weird to say, but I was excited because I had been meandering through Paris with a bunch of adventures this whole time and finally, it all made sense now: my depression, my anxiety, my lack of progress. All of it was validated and revealed and clarified in Dorian and now, through her, I could get to the bottom of it. I never wanted this to happen, that's not what I'm saying, would never have challenged myself or anyone to this. But now that it was here we could finally be real. Dorian could finally be real. I felt free and open, like Paris had just given me an opportunity to be human and I would take it. Before I had had to be a marble statue on a pilaster for so long, some writer demi-god, thought I had wanted that and needed that. But now I could just be human, imperfect, broken, raw, real and I felt free for the first time in years and it felt like an adventure, the best adventure I had been challenged to yet.

．　．　．

THEY RELEASED Dorian from the hospital. They said she was okay, not a threat to try it again. Dorian's sister flew in from California, and we made plans to all have brunch at Dorian's. Talia and Joy would cook and Dorian could rest among friends who didn't need her to be perfect for them.

"Wait, only two stops?" I said to Talia as we got off at Cluny. "I didn't realize she lived this close."

We walked a few blocks until we found her building. Across the street was a bakery crowded with colorful treats, blue, yellow, green meringues the size of your head. Her building was a thin medieval-looking place just down the street from Notre Dame and a block from Shakespeare and Co. We had passed this street so many times and had no idea our only friend in Paris lived here.

I got angry again because she had lived so close and why had she always made such a big deal about meeting us? Why hadn't she told us where she lived? Why hadn't she invited us over? We were so close! But it was stupid because I knew why. Paris was all-consuming. Why think about friends when you have this architecture, the nearness of art, streetside cafés for every afternoon, and so many books to read? Yes we were lonely, but I often felt as we were going out to see someone we knew, wouldn't it be great to stay home? Or just go out by ourselves somewhere, just us? I wanted friends, but I also resented my need for them. The shyness of this city seeps into you.

But Dorian's suicide attempt shattered all of that. We were not in normal time anymore. We were all experiencing something else, something liminal, and all our plans got placed outside of that time. We were bound up. Our time was all promised to each other and in the midst of those promises we were also oddly free. Free to be who we were.

We walked up Dorian's steps. So many steps, many worn down so they were more like ramps. She was in the attic room of a five story building and there was no elevator.

"No wonder she was so depressed," I said. "I would never leave my house if I lived up here."

We knocked on the hunched door at the top of the stairs. Joy opened it and we smiled and hugged. We met Dorian's sister, whom I honestly have no memory of except that she was odd and kind of funny. They didn't have orange juice for the mimosas, and so I went to get more. Down the dozens of slopey steps, across the street, down the avenue, into the shop, and back. Up up up so many steps. I had wondered how Dorian could have afforded that spot in the 5th and so close to Notre Dame until I went up all those steps.

"I saw the bakery across the street. It looked amazing," I said setting down the orange juice. Talia opened it and poured it into the glasses already half full of sparkling wine.

"None for you?" I said, as Dorian grabbed the one sans-wine.

"My throat's still feeling raw," she said.

I looked at her, trying to acknowledge the pain in my look. She shrugged and went about helping Talia with the breakfast and I looked around her place.

Dorian's "apartment" was a little low-ceilinged studio that was pretty miserable except for the view out of the small window of the cathedral. She had a guitar and an easel with a rough watercolor of a woman in a blue dress.

When we had first seen Dorian I had found her blog and seen pictures of these things, read about how she had painted that woman. She had melancholic and sophisticated pictures of her shadowed form looking out the window of her garret. They looked so artistic, then, but in our context they were also tragic. These were not enough to keep you alive, they said. Not this view. Not the ability to paint in your Parisian garret. Not your guitar. Not your tiny white kitchen. Not your éclairs and tea cakes and head-sized turquoise meringues. These still won't satisfy you. And I felt out for my own vanity then and felt how insatiable it was, like a deep darkness inside me full of shade and ash. I set it aside and picked up the guitar. It had been a while. Mars was half-napping in his stroller and I sang to him.

"Swing like a wrecking ball, like the heart of God what a mystery," I sang it to Mars, but really to me and to Dorian and Talia and to all of us. "Filled with the wedding feast for the snakes and bees with the angel teeth. Swing." The room had nice acoustics and though I sang softly it carried, a low hum that reverberated the room. "Come and carry us, come and marry us to the blushing circus king," I sang and I could tell as someone who has played long enough that they were listening and it was meaning something to them. The conversations were still going but softer now and then they stopped altogether and there was just the sound of chopping and pans clinking and my playing.

"Fire come and carry us, make us shine or make us rust, tell us that you care for us, we need to hear a word for us. Let your body stand with us or let our rags be turned to dust. Oh chariot you swing for us we think that you can carry all of us."[1]

That lullaby I had sung for Mars so many times soothing my heart, soothing all of our hearts.

"And we will become, a happy ending. A happy ending."

I finished the song and set the guitar down but the room was still ringing with the music but it was in our heads now, in our hearts.

We ate and drank coffee and mimosas. I did dishes.

Later, just before we were supposed to go, Dorian came up to me. "Thank you for that song. It was lovely."

"It felt good to play," I said. "I'm glad you liked it."

For weeks I had been emailing Dorian to schedule job shadowing for my adventure. I had tried to accomplish this adventure, and I felt guilty then about not really finishing it. I feel a little guilty even now. Perhaps in some ways I did job shadow a chef, not because I learned her job but because I learned her life, and for a writer what is more essential than that? But the truth was I had given up on job shadowing Dorian weeks before that. She gave many excuses for the missed emails or missed appointments, but we were never able to work it out. Now I guess I understood why. Dorian knew Paris in a way I didn't, in a way I wanted to. It wasn't until later, years later, that I realized I was actually drawn to Dorian because I *was* her. Dorian was *me*, just a few months earlier on the journey. She had come to Paris to experience culture and sophistication and find a new life, new, better routines, finally accomplish her purpose, perhaps. And just as I had, she found that the sophistication happened but it didn't satisfy. Her Instagram photos and blog posts got better, but who can live on likes and comments alone? I thought all these things would make me happy. Dorian thought all these things would make her happy. But instead we were just getting more and more depressed. More and more lost. But I didn't know just how lost she was—and perhaps I would have gotten lost too, given enough time. If I hadn't had Talia, and if I had been there eight months longer, who knows what choices I could have made?

· · ·

WE HAD dinner all together later that night at a little basque place.

"Man," said Talia, looking at the menu. "I wish we had found places like this sooner. It's so *cheap*."

"It's so good too," said Dorian.

We sat out on the patio and it was warm and crowded and all the girls passed around the baby. I asked the waiter what to order and he told me a dish and it came out with green peppers and onions and meat and I was surprised because I had never seen peppers in French food but it was delicious even though I have never liked green peppers. I was still hungry afterwards so I finished Talia's and some of Joy's plate too.

We were feeling happy and safe together, and so when Talia was talking to Joy and Dorian's sister, I turned to Dorian who was sitting across from me.

"How are you feeling?" I asked her.

"Tired. But better."

"Do you think you'll want to try again?" I asked.

"No," she said. "I didn't ever think I would try a first time. They say it never goes all the way away, though. That it can always come back. I know I need to be careful and make sure I'm not isolating myself."

"Do you think you'll go back home?" I asked.

"I don't *want* to. I might go to Spain for a little while."

"That would be nice. When we first met . . . I felt like you looked pretty beat up."

"You saw that?" she asked.

"Yeah."

"Well. You were right," she said.

"I'm sorry. Paris can be hard."

"Yeah, it can."

And then Joy said something funny and we turned and

smiled in her direction and soon the evening was over and everyone felt good even though we'd come out of so much.

That was the best night in Paris. There were a few very good nights in Paris and many dull nights but that was the night when I felt like my heart was full.

There were still a few more adventures to be had, though. After all, I still hadn't made it into the real catacombs. Oh, and my grandma would be there soon.

Challenge no. 8: Friend

Visit a friend just to see how they're doing. Consider dropping in unexpectedly. If that's not possible, only give them a few hours' warning just to make it fun. Don't stay long, but make plans to see each other again soon.

9

ROMANCE

Romance your wife in an unexpected way. I picture this looking like you bringing her along on your day of adventures (get a babysitter that she trusts perhaps) and plant someone near the end of the day who will tell you they really need your help, or they have to show you something and they will take you two to a beautifully set table overlooking the romantic sights of Paris or something. (Submitted by Ross B.)

Dorian left with Joy for Spain to recuperate. We were alone again. But the city was waking up. The sun was going down later. The days were warmer. It was springtime in Paris.

"Did you think any more about what we talked about?" Talia asked me one night after I put Mars to bed.

"What do you mean?"

"About our big fight?"

"Oh. Right. . . ." Did I want to get into this? Could I just keep hiding, keep putting off this conversation? Everything from my experience with Dorian told me I could but there would be consequences. I took a deep breath. "I just think you have expectations I'm never going to be able to meet. I don't—"

"I think we should take a sex class," she interrupted.

"Huh?"

"A sex class. There's this online course by John Gottman. And we could do it from Paris. We could start now, actually."

A sex class. We had come to the city of love, one of the most romantic places in the world, and Talia thought we needed a class to teach us how to have better sex.

"You really think we need to take a class about that?"

"It's not just about sex. It's about intimacy. Just watch the video."

"Ugghghg," I said. "Fine. Show me."

She handed me the laptop and sat beside me while I watched it. There was an older, bearded man wearing a red turtleneck and a belly on a stool. His wife, an older woman with thick curly hair almost to her belly button, sat next to him. Both were psychologists, so they knew things, but they were just about the least cool people ever. It was even worse watching them talk about sex and intimacy. Can you imagine? Old unattractive people talking about their sex life, and how *your* sex life should be? It was horrible.

And yet.

Gottman began the video saying he could predict whether a couple would stay together or get divorced with over ninety percent accuracy. He said he had been working with couples for over forty years to create lasting, fulfilling, and satisfying relationships.

I didn't want to get a divorce. Of course I wanted better sex. Most of all, I wanted Talia to be genuinely happy, and she just wasn't and hadn't been for a long time. Maybe this was the concrete thing she needed to help her do that. But I also resented the idea of having to take a class on it.

All I wanted was to appear calm, confident, and most of all, competent. Most of the time, I felt like the opposite of all of those things. It didn't help that I felt anxious, insecure, and incompetent in my writing and in each of the adventures. Now I was feeling that way with Talia, too. The image I was trying to project was shattering. I could either hold on to it, or let it crumble completely.

"What do you think?" Talia asked.

"Fine. Let's do it."

TALIA, Mars, and I left the metro at Bir-Hakeim and followed the signs to Champ de Mars, turned right, then right again, and finally found ourselves underneath that most quintessential of Parisian sights.

I had walked to the Eiffel Tower a few times, once on my own in my explorations of the city and once with Bethany. But tonight was a special occasion, the 125th anniversary of its completion. I hadn't followed all of Ross's directions because now that Dorian was gone, we didn't know a single babysitter in all of Paris. BUT I did pack a bottle of wine, seven different kinds of charcuterie and cheeses, and two beautiful baguettes from Gérard Mulot for the best picnic under the Eiffel Tower ever.

We set out our picnic on the southeast side of the tower and I lay back on the grass, which was still cool and slightly wet from the long winter, and looked up to the top of the tower which looked so small and insignificant here beneath it.

It was early evening still, but already there were hundreds of people in the park, some on blankets like us, others riding bikes or walking dogs. We let Mars crawl around and we drank our wine and ate.

"Should we do our questions?" I asked.

"Sure. Do you want to?"

"Not really. But we can."

I pulled out my printed sheet of questions from the sex class. As awkward as it was to hear two old psychologists talk about sex, I honestly wished they were there with us then, if only to help us get through all the questions. There were a hundred in all, and they were just about the most uncomfortable questions in the world. For example:

"Many men say they like masturbation if they have not come during intercourse. They like being held while they masturbate. Do you agree with that?" *Well, no I don't agree, but I also never want to talk about masturbation, ever.*

"What is it like when you have an orgasm? What are the physical sensations? What do you feel?" *Um . . . it feels good. But please let's not talk about it, ever ever.*

"Do you feel pressure to have sex with me? What can I do to make that better?" *Umm . . . maybe? But I think I'm feeling more pressure having this conversation.*

"When you initiate sex, what do you usually feel?" *So . . . that's an interesting question. And I think we should definitely talk about it. But can we please just look at the beautiful scenery for a while. It's the 125th birthday of the Eiffel Tower. Isn't that amazing? Oh, the question? Yes, maybe we can come back to that in a moment, after enjoying the scenery . . . for just . . . a little . . . longer.*

"Tell me honestly, are there things I do that help you like your body? What could I do to make you feel better about your body?" *Stop talking. I would like my body so much better if you just stop talking.*

"What sexual fantasies do you enjoy? Can you share them with me?" *Dear God please . . . the SCENERY. PARIS!*

"I want to talk to you about kissing, touching, caressing, and love talk. What about this thing that people call "foreplay" do you like the best?" *AGHHGHGH!*

"Do you ever think of or want to have sex with other people?" *AGHHGHGHGHGHGHGHGHGH!!!*

"What are your feelings about anal sex in general, giving and receiving it?" *I think I'm dying. Nope, I think I'm already dead. Please let me be dead.*

When you've been married for a few years, especially if you have kids, you look around one day and think, "Oh, this is it. I had a good run. There were some exciting moments, some bad moments, but now I've arrived. Life will always be the same now. And I just better live with it."

Some people respond to that by focusing on their careers or their kids. Others rebel against it and have affairs and blow their marriages apart. Some people find religion or meditation and just try to be content with sameness. The novelty is gone, so you just dig your trench and go to war against your desire so you can stay where you are and never move.

I hated those questions. I'm reading them again now and hate them all over again. But I also recognized the adventure in them too. I'd been doing this for awhile now, this adventure thing, and I realized the same level of discomfort I had for approaching a guy doing muay thai on Rue de Buci I also had when Talia asked me one of those questions. It was uncomfortable and annoying and kind of gut-level painful, but it was also leading me to someplace new, someplace risky; there was a goal here that I didn't fully understand but I thought it might be good.

Should I be honest? Should I lie? Hedge my bets? I thought about this again and again.

It would be so easy. Sitting there having a picnic below the Eiffel Tower. All I had to do was say something that sounded good. Or something that was believable at least.

It would just be a little lie. A little omission.

And then I could hide again.

Show the face that I wanted.

But then, in a few months, we'd be back to where we started, wouldn't we?

I was lonely in Paris. No doubt. Both Talia and I were.

Half of that was because we didn't have any friends. The other half was because we weren't really being honest with each other. Or really, because I wasn't being honest. Wasn't that what Talia had been trying to tell me all those times?

Maybe this is half the reason, at least, I wanted to leave that small town life. To escape myself. To flee any responsibility to honesty. In a small town, you can't be anyone but who you've been in the past. I wanted to be so much more, but how could I do that there?

Maybe. Instead. I needed to be honest. Maybe. Instead. I needed to talk about how I felt about initating sex and how my orgasms felt and whether I liked my anus being stimulated. I mean, some of those things I could have been okay with never experiencing or talking about ever, but maybe this was an adventure, an adventure I didn't have to be in Paris to accomplish; I just had to be alive and awake and myself to accomplish. Maybe I should have been listening to Talia, whom I loved, Talia, my best friend who made Paris, my whole life really, possible and so much better, maybe I should have been listening to her this whole time and not just a bunch of people I didn't even know, not that they weren't important—not that you, dear reader, aren't important—just that you're not the most important, and really, if you are that's not fair to you or me or anyone really.

Maybe I would never stop wanting the approval/intrigue/attention of others, but I also needed, truly *needed*, Talia, who grounded me, who made me the best version of myself, my Talia who could help me be me in the midst of it all.

God I was so tired in that field underneath the Eiffel Tower. I was so tired and so done. Tired of projecting this image of competence, calmness, confidence into the world. Tired enough to start telling Talia the truth.

I did. All of it. It sucked. I felt so uncomfortable.

Mars played in the grass and made friends with all the random strangers and Talia and I talked about our sex life and everything about us really and I felt it all slipping away from me, all that image I had tried to uphold. I almost cried, I felt so vulnerable when we walked home in the dusk; we skipped the metro; it was only a few miles. Walking through the 7th to the 6th, past all the embassies and government buildings and cafés. Past Coutume and Le Nemrod and Le Marché. By the end I was exhausted, but I also felt clean. Whole. Like I was just me and that was enough. Would it be enough forever, I didn't know. But it was enough for now. For Talia.

Challenge no. 9: Questions

The adventure into another's heart isn't easy, is often the longest journey you experience in your life, and contains great risk! However, the destination is worth it.

To begin the journey toward the heart of your partner,

discuss these questions with your spouse or significant other.

1. Do you like to be touched? If so, where do you like to be touched? Do we touch enough? If not, how could we touch more?
2. Do you like masturbating yourself?
3. How do you feel when I masturbate you?
4. Do you enjoy oral sex?
5. What do you like or dislike about oral sex?
6. What is it like when you have an orgasm? What are the physical sensations? What do you feel?
7. There is a saying that some men want sex to feel close and some men only want sex when they already feel close. Which one do you think is true of you? What is true of us? If you could change things, would you?
8. What is the feeling of being aroused like for you? Do you feel wanted? Do you feel alive? Is there urgency? Is there a sense of calm? Do you feel desired? Loved? Tell me what this is like for you.
9. After you climax, do you feel satisfied? What do you feel like you need from me in that space? Tenderness and closeness? Are you sleepy or do you feel energized?
10. Do you feel that I pursue you? Or have we stopped? What can I do to make that better?

Then reflect together on what surprised you about your partner's responses. Did their answers make you feel closer or more distant?

TRIPE

Eat Tripe. (From Alice S.)

❧

I went to cafés and wrote.

I went to Café de la Marie and ordered a *noisette* and forget to say *s'il vous plait*. I had my favorite waiter. He was old, frumpy, but very serious and had Buddy Holly glasses not because it was an affectation but because he probably found them at a thrift store. I drank half of my noisette immediately and then let it sit until it got cold. It was cold outside and I was sitting on the opposite side of the table from the windows. I had been cold in many cafés in Paris because I liked to sit by the windows or else outside and watch people on the street but today I wanted to be warm.

To inspire me I read some of Mark Twain's *The Innocents Abroad*, his travelogue as he took a ship from Boston around the countries in the Mediteranean and then back. It was by far his bestselling book during his lifetime. We remember

Twain as the author of *Huck Finn* and *Tom Sawyer* or maybe as "the father of American literature" as Faulkner called him, but during his lifetime he was known as the guy who wrote a travelogue about going to Egypt and the Holy Land and sometimes gave funny speeches. I read *The Innocents Abroad*, trying to understand why people loved it so much, and I thought, *This is very funny and witty but also so exaggerated and fake, like a caricature even if it's a caricature by a master.* I stopped reading and thought about Mark Twain and wondered if he had stopped writing after his travelogue whether he would have been forgotten.

At the table next to me were three men having a meeting. One of them looked like a caricature of a pretentious French maître d'. He was very thin and had a long nose and wavy hair combed back and best of all a pencil mustache. He was wearing Adidas, though, which kind of ruined the joke.

I tried to write. *You must keep your fingers moving,* I thought. *You want to look out the window at Rue de Canettes where you live. You want to look into the mirror through which you can see a police car stopped beside a man on a motorcycle. You want to watch your old, serious waiter, but you must keep your fingers moving. That's the only way you can write something worthwhile. It's easier than you're making it; just keep your fingers moving.*

Pencil mustache guy crossed his legs and sharpened his pencil into the saucer, then started writing in a notebook. The man across from him looked like Mr. Bennet from *Pride and Prejudice* (the BBC version of course) and he's writing mathematical formulas on a napkin. They were professors, then, perhaps discussing a proof? He was drinking Chartreuse and tonic, and yes I totally had to look that up because I'd never seen anyone drink a weird green liqueur with tonic. The last of the group had a very round belly with his pants above his waist and for some reason reminded me of a Russian egg doll.

The dark haired waiter went into the kitchen and came back with a plate and sat down at a table and began to eat his lunch. He had a whole baguette and a plate of smoked salmon and an orangina soda. He ran out of mustard and went back into the kitchen for more. *Why is he so tan? It's March. Is he Italian? Or does he go to tanning salons?*

What did this all mean? I thought. What did this café mean? What did these mathematicians beside me mean? What did Paris and what did France mean?

Was this a story?

Was this *my* story?

I wanted something to happen, something worth writing about. If nothing happened, I wanted to be able to make something up at the very least.

God what should I do?

Keep your fingers moving. That's the only thing there is.

I went to Le Rostand and there was a cat perched on top of the table where all the menus were stacked. A man who looked like Vladimir Putin blew it a kiss and then he paid his tab and left, but when he crossed the street there was a Mini convertible with four beautiful women in it. He shouted something in French and they laughed and he pretended to climb in with them for some grand adventure and they were all laughing.

I went to Coutume and ordered a cortado. The Canadian girl who never talked to me brought it out and it had a design of a tiny branch with three little berries in the foam.

I tried to write and then wrote emails for a while and then I wrote about the two old men who I saw helping each other cross the street while I was walking to the café. They both had canes and one of them was a little more stooped than the other. They wore cardigans and hats of course. The stooped one was named Larry, and he had his arm around François's shoulder. I just made those names up but they looked right. François had has arm around Larry's waist to hold him up. They were walking the opposite way from me and I smiled at them as I passed but I think they were too focused on helping each other down the street to smile back.

What was my story? Was that my story?

How do you know if you have any stories to tell? I was smart and I knew things, but what does that matter if you can't tell a story? I wondered if I should just write textbooks. I wondered if I should become an editor.

A man with an enviable Rasputinesque beard came into the café. You couldn't help but watch him because of the beard. There was a very pretty girl waiting for him and they kissed cheeks and sat at a table across from me. I overheard her talking in French with a raspy voice. Rasputin had bad teeth but a great hat.

This is what you do in a Parisian café. It's why Parisians don't need very many friends, because they can just go to a café and watch these people. *If I were Rasputin's friend*, I thought, *would that be a good life or a bad life?*

I read an email from my mom, who had found me a writing gig in Santa Barbara. I thought about summer in Santa Barbara, foggy and sixty degrees in June and then seventy degrees and perfect in July. I could play volleyball with Danny on the beach in the mornings and then go to Sly's with my dad for drinks. I could write at French Press Café and Lucky Llama. But then I realized I was thinking about the next trip while I was in Paris and when you're in Paris you should be thinking about Paris.

It was late afternoon now and there was a dance remix of a Madonna song playing. The barista started to dance and he was very good.

Later he approached me.

"I'm trying to think of a name," he said.

"Of what?"

"Of this drink," he said setting a coffee down in front of me. "Do you want to try it?"

I sipped and it tasted like nutmeg and apple and other spices, like an apple turnover in a latte.

"I like it! Thank you!"

"You're a writer. You have to help me with names."

I said a few names and he didn't like any of them.

I went to Le Rostand and drank my noisette without sugar because it made it bitter and so I would have to drink it more slowly. I had painted here with Pauline and she had told me a lot of publishers come here. I sat outside in the sun and I began to sweat and I realized it was the first time I had sweated in Paris without a coat.

What should I write about today? I thought. *Today is about fun. What fun thing can I write?*

That morning I had rented a Vélib bike and tried to ride to Notre Dame but got lost because I wasn't sure how to turn left on a four-lane boulevard past buses and motorcycles. I learned there are two highways along the Seine and they are both one way and if you get on the one that goes the wrong way you will be in trouble. I had to try a different route through side streets and then got to the bridge on Île de la Cité right next to Notre Dame but couldn't figure out how to turn onto the bridge and so had to make a huge loop and finally made it to the cathedral and was very relieved.

Was that a publisher over there, the one who looked like Newman from Seinfeld?

I was tired of publishers and their false condolence letters. I never liked publishers but if they said they wanted to publish me I would say yes. It's just the running after them that I hated.

The waiters here wore jeans instead of tuxes. Their coats were baggy and simple and they ended up looking like miners, I thought.

It was almost time for me to go home and relieve Talia who was always exhausted by that time. The baby would probably be awake and it was a very small apartment and he crawled over everything, even your head, and he pulled at your computer cables and mashed the keys. It was cute sometimes. That was what being a parent was about, enduring the many annoying moments because the cute ones brought so much joy.

An older couple beside me waved to the waiter, who came over and took their order. The man had a backpack and a map in his coat pocket and I knew they were tourists even though they looked so French. The waiter brought him a Corona without lime (really? a Corona?) and the couple studied the bottle as if it was an award winning craft beer and I wondered again why Europeans were obsessed with clear beer.

I realized I had written four pages by that point and it was all complete crap that no one would ever want to read.

Back at home, I connected my phone to the wifi and found out my brother-in law had gotten engaged and everyone was talking about it. My sister-in-law had gotten engaged in Ireland a few weeks before, and it felt like my family was in the process of becoming something new, something better, but I was removed from it, above it, in Paris. I missed home.

I was back at Le Rostand. The sun was in my eyes and I

was feeling sleepy. *Should I leave?* I thought. I closed my eyes and nearly fell asleep but I caught myself.

I wanted to spread a giant white sheet on the grass across the street at the Luxembourg Gardens. I wanted to drink a double espresso and then fall asleep and wake up half an hour later ready to write. A woman beside me ordered an apricot tart and it looked delicious. All the desserts here looked delicious. Did the publishers meet inside or here outside? How much did that tart cost?

Back at Café Sainte-Marie a man with thin black hair that looked dyed came in and joined pencil mustache man and Mr. Bennet. Pencil mustache man, whom I'd grown to like, stood up and shook his hand and half-bowed, so he must've been important. He sat down and they talked for a while and then he noticed me watching and I looked away but out of the corner of my eye I saw him staring. It didn't feel hostile, though, just curious.

You do not feel more alive while writing in a cafe in Paris. I thought I would but you don't. Making art is supposed to feel like being fully alive and fully awake, but you do not feel more awake when writing in Paris, although the cold helps. You do feel more distracted. You are in the best, most inspiring place in the world to write, so why can't you write something that is the best, the most inspired.

I realized I was writing like another writer, in second person with lots of conjunctions, but it was flowing and I had written ten pages without thinking and I didn't want it to stop. I wanted to write my own story in my own voice but the words were coming and I was in rhythm. The weight was gone, all the expectation was gone, and I was cold and awake. Was it worth sounding like another writer so that I could write at all? Could I be satisfied with that? Of course not. But could I try?

My espresso was quite good but it was gone too quickly and I didn't have money for more.

Was this my story? Where was my story? Yes, this was writing. Yes, my fingers were moving. But was it any good?

A writer friend texted me. I didn't answer at first, trying to stay focused, but then I did. I thought of Hemingway and all the writer friends he made in Paris and I realized that would not happen to me here.

It was five o'clock and nearly time to go home and I had written twelve pages but I didn't know if they were any good. What else? What else needed to be written?

I went to Le Nemrod and did not write. I went with Talia. Mars was quiet for once.

I ordered the tripe and I was brave about it all until it came out. It was surrounded by beautiful golden brown potatoes and dark green hand-picked vegetables from the heart of France but it was pale and wrapped in a string to keep all the thin stringy cow stomach together. I thought about not eating it, but what would they say. And honestly it didn't look so bad. I might even like it. That would be the worst thing of all, to like it, and then I would have to be the weirdo who eats stomach and brain and all the other body parts that no one in my country is interested in.

I almost gave up at that point. Who would know? I would say I ate it and that would have been that.

I felt so tired of these adventures.

I cut off a corner and put it in my mouth. It was soft and a little chewy but also savory and salty and if I didn't think about it too much it was delicious. I ate another bite, bigger this time, and thought, *I could see how people get into this*. I ate half and then all of a sudden I was full and couldn't eat any more.

The couple beside us, when they were through with

their food, turned toward each other whispering secrets and touching all over and stealing kisses. You do what that couple was doing in America and people will look at you like you're crazy and your family will say, "Ew gross." Or at least they used to do that to Talia and me.

Talia and I held hands and I kissed her and she looked at me smiling that way that she used to when we were first married.

Perhaps I was starting to understand Paris after all.

At Café de la Marie the professors were getting up to leave but I kept writing.

What was it? What was it? What was I looking for, that final thing to write? I don't know. I don't know.

Most of my writing time I felt I was looking for something, some other story that I hadn't found yet. How would I find it?

And then a cat came in. It walked right through the door and I just saw its tail from the corner of my eye and it startled me so much I stopped writing. Was it really there? Was I just imagining it?

I decided the cat must be hiding somewhere underneath the tables when the dark haired waiter comes to collect all the professors' glasses from their empty table, but the cat didn't come out. It must have been feasting on the crumbs of smoked salmon from the dark haired waiter's lunch. And then it was there again, walking out the door.

I looked around but no one else had noticed.

I wrote at Coutume and then when I was getting up to leave I was saying goodbye to my dancing barista friend when I realized I felt comfortable and at home finally. I was supposed to leave Paris in less than two weeks, so it was a bad time to feel at home, but I felt that way.

I paid my check to the Canadian girl who never talked to

me and she started talking to me. She was from Montreal, she told me, and she was going to school in Paris and working at the café to pay the rent and no she didn't have any Parisian friends either, except of course for her boyfriend who was Parisian but his friends were standoffish to her because that's how the French are and her rent was way too high because housing is the worst in Paris. I left feeling like I'd finally made it.

I didn't know it then, but that would be the last time I would go to Coutume.

I wrote in the cafés of Paris but the problem with writing like this was you could not know the end. There was no end to a story that was happening to you right then. It is only the stories you've already lived through that have endings and those only have endings because you trick your mind into coming up with them.

I drank half of my coffee and then let the rest grow cold. I wrote until I was exhausted, until I didn't want to go home but I didn't want to be in that café anymore, until I had written enough to not want to read it the next day because I knew it was terrible, although there might be some good pieces in there that I could make into something useful, although I knew making something useful would take a long time.

I would close my computer and sit for a little longer just watching and not thinking of anything.

Then I would look at the waiter until he came over and I would give him my five euro and get my change and go home to my wife and baby who would crawl over my shoulders and my lap and through all the cleaning supplies until the morning when I would do this again. Would I have a story tomorrow, I would think. I felt like I was always between stories, never in the middle of them, and most of all, I wanted that feeling to go away but it wouldn't. All you can do is say thank you when the story comes. To say thank you and be awake, perhaps sit in the cold for awhile, until the next story comes. And then to call your waiter and pay the check and go home prepared to do it again the next day, if you get the chance.

Challenge no. 10: Appetizing

Go to a nice restaurant. It can be fancy but it doesn't have to be. It *should* have a reputation for being thoughtful, even innovative about how they prepare food.

Then, order the item that sounds the *least* appetizing to you.

Food is an adventure, but you can't have an adventure without risk!

Did you like it? Or is it exactly as horrible as you anticipated?

11

MUSEUMS

*Visit ten museums in Paris. Write about what you see, as well as
the comments you exchanged when you were looking at each of
the exhibitions in those museums. (Submitted by Paul N.)*

～

Three days before we were set to leave Paris, my family arrived—my parents, Grandma, and Grandma's fiancé. It was Grandma and her eighty-fifth birthday that started this whole thing for us, so it was appropriate she was there at the end. Upon their arrival, Talia, Mars, and I almost instantly transformed from residents of the city to tour guides, ready to see and show every site in Paris.

"Should we eat lunch at Les Deux Magots?" I asked my father. "You know James Joyce used to eat there with his family. Actually, he and Hemingway drank sherry there once. Hemingway wrote about it in *A Sun Also Rises*. It's one of the original great cafés in Paris. It's a bit expensive, but you should probably eat there at least once."

Somehow he agreed. I *might* have left out just how expensive it was. Oops.

We sat inside, under a gold chandelier, not far from the plaque that says, "Hemingway wrote here." The table was made of rich wood and the seats covered in red leather. A statue of a saint was looking at me as I ordered a simple sandwich that was still almost twenty euro. We ordered wine. The waiter wore a tuxedo, of course, and a much more distinguished one than the old, rumpled tuxedos worn by the waiters at Café Mairie.

Everyone was excited to be in Paris. Even I was excited, not just because my family was there but because I could finally be a tourist. We had put off seeing most of the museums and sights and now we could finally enjoy them all.

Talia told them about all our favorite things to do and made plans for all the places we would soon go to see. I chimed in from time to time but mostly I held Mars and thought of our time in Paris which was coming to an end.

Had it been worth it? Had we actually accomplished anything?

I bounced Mars on my knee until my mother took him out for a walk. I drank the rest of my wine, holding it in my mouth letting the smooth, earthy taste sink down into the pores of my tongue. When the waiter came by, I ordered a *noisette*.

Another café checked off the list, I thought. Only a million more, a lifetime worth, to go.

Those days, Paris was beautiful and sunny and warm without being hot. We ate out all the time, now that we had other people to pick up the baby and keep him quiet (and sometimes to pick up the check). We showed them how to take the metro and how to cross the street like a Parisian and what food to order and where all the best things could be found—the best bread, the best *chocolat*, the best wine, the best views.

We did all the things: we took a river cruise at night and saw the Eiffel Tower shimmer in the night, and of course we went to the museums, all the museums we didn't have the time or money for when we were on our own: the Louvre, the Arc de Triomphe, Orsay, the Pantheon, Organgerie, SacréCœur, Luxembourg, Opéra Garnier, and of course Notre Dame.

Maybe it was because my family were so new to Paris and I was, by this time, so comfortable, or maybe it was because we were finally around people we knew for longer than 24 hours, or maybe it was that I truly was finding my place there, but I was finally feeling at home in Paris.

The morning after they arrived, we took our usual route up Rue de Seine, past the galleries, through the arch at the Académie des Beaux-Arts, and over Pont des Arts bridge to the Louvre.

What can you say about the Louvre that has not been said? It is big and overwhelming and it is hard not to feel crushed by all the culture in that place. I stood at the back of the mob around the Mona Lisa. I saw the Greek Venus, Michaelangelo's slaves—which were amazing—Winged Victory, the two Vermeers, the giant Delacroix of the July Revolution not far from the even-more-giant painting of the coronation of Napoleon, the famous da Vinci and the not-so-famous da Vinci, and so many more. They were all beautiful, but what I loved the most was imagining the lives of the kings and queens who lived in that palace, to put myself in the shoes of their power and know how intoxicating it would have been and also how perilous.

After a true French lunch at La Palette, a restaurant on

Rue de Seine with a pleasant garden patio that we had
passed a dozen times but could never afford (thanks again,
Dad), we headed for the Musée d'Orsay.

Thomas Merton hated Orsay because it was in a train
station, which reminded him of busyness and crowds and
noise, all of which he despised, but I loved the openness of
it, the way you could go up to the balconies and look out
and see a dozen of the most beautiful sculptures in the
world. I loved the way the museum led you from the realists
and classicists of the Salon to the Impressionist revolution. I
loved going up into the "attic" and seeing all the Van Goghs,
the Monets, the Degas, the Cezannes all in one place which
you could never see together in any other museum in the
world. I loved it and felt full and sad afterward, like after
eating the best meal and feeling empty because it's over.

From there we went back to Rue des Canettes for an
early dinner at Boucherie Roulièr, a restaurant and
butchery with modern, delicious food and a long family
tradition. And then back out.

The first stop was the Eiffel Tower, or rather a perfect
view of the Eiffel Tower from the Trocadéro.

Looking across the Seine at that quintessential Paris
landmark, I came back to that question that had been
haunting me in Les Deux Magots. Had Paris been worth it?
Had we actually accomplished anything here? I tried to
remember why we came to Paris in the first place. What
had I been looking for that I thought I would find here? I
remembered feeling like I was in a rut. I remembered being
hemmed in by the small life I was living and desperate for
something new. I remembered that the passion and excitement I once had about being a writer had completely faded.
I had been *writing*, but I felt like a fraud. At the same time, I
had dreamed about traveling for years but I wasn't traveling,

I couldn't get Talia to *want* to travel with me, and even if I could have convinced her, we also had a new baby which made any kind of travel seem impossible. Worst of all, Talia had been unhappy. She hadn't felt connected, she hadn't felt loved. I knew then I had needed to fix it, my marriage, my career, my life, and Paris seem to be the best way to do it.

Did it work?

Not at first, no.

Coming to Paris had gotten me out of my rut, but then I fell into a worse one. I tried to live a new lifestyle, but then got stuck in bad habits (looking at you, Sudoku). I accomplished what I had always wanted to do, to travel the world and write, but I also found true escape is impossible, especially when trying to escape yourself.

I wasn't all that happier having been to Paris.

And perhaps that wasn't the point.

Perhaps it was too much to ask a city to make me happy, to fulfill all my needs and make all my dreams come true.

Perhaps it was enough that Paris had made me a better husband, a better father, a better writer, a better person.

It was the one thing that I didn't really want that saved me. Even though I had fought against it, what I had wanted, what I had *needed*, was an adventure. And that's exactly what I got in Paris.

In Paris, I had gone from a too-small life with little risk to an uncomfortably big life with *so* much risk, so many chances for failure (and I *did* fail!), and most of all, so many opportunities to grow.

In Paris, I wrote, failed at writing, played a lot of Sudoku, and then finally fell into a writing habit that had produced nearly half of a book. I didn't always feel like a writer, but I *did* stop caring as much. I *was* a writer, my feelings be damned. Who did I need to prove it to anymore? I had proven it to myself.

In Paris, I hadn't just traveled, I had proven that my family and I *could* travel with a baby. Being a parent didn't mean I was trapped with a house with a white picket fence and a two-car garage and a too-big mortgage and a day job I didn't really enjoy. We could live anywhere, we could go anywhere. It might not be easy and we might need to be better prepared next time, maybe find a place where we could have community so we wouldn't be as lonely, but we could figure it out.

In Paris, Talia and I fought and bickered and were distant from each other and fought some more until we found ourselves closer than we had ever been. I knew so many couples who instead of working out their problems found better and better ways of distracting themselves from their problems. Paris didn't allow us to do that. We eventually had to confront them. *I* had to confront them. I also knew that we were closer because of Paris, and that we would continue to get closer because of the work we had done there.

Always be growing. Always be taking risks. Always be setting goals that will be too high for you to achieve at least half the time. Forget happiness. Commit to adventure.

What adventures are you, dear reader, setting out for today?

Who will you take with you?

I looked around at my family. My father who was looking out at the Eiffel Tower and smiling. My grandmother who was eighty-five years old, breathing a little heavy from our walk, but still ready to get back on the metro and head out to our next adventure. My mother pushing the stroller with Mars. Mars, who was looking at a Paris he would never remember but would always have as a kind of inheritance. I looked at Talia and held her hand and smiled and knew that even though this was the last time we'd see the Eiffel Tower on this visit, it was just the beginning of a lifetime of memories of Paris.

This is what I wanted, what I always wanted, to be going on an adventure with the people I loved the most. Paris wasn't perfect, but it was good, and I was ready to experience it all one last time.

THE NEXT MORNING we all got up early and made the short walk to Gérard Mulot for *pains au chocolat* which everyone groaned over as we ate them in Grandma's hotel dining area. Then we headed for the train station.

There were two things I was looking forward to about going to Versaille. The first was the place itself, partially out of a desire to see the huge estate where Louis XIV attracted the best, brightest, and most of all, richest of France. I wanted to get into the Sun King's head. I was fascinated by Louis XIV. He began his reign in the middle of a civil war, afraid for his life and for everything his family had built. And yet he managed to take a kingdom in turmoil and turn it into the leading power not just of Europe but of all the world, and hung on to wield that power for over seventy years. How did he do it? What kind of person do you have to become to draw a whole nation, a whole continent to you?

The other thing I was looking forward to about Versailles was the chance at riding in the "painted train," a train that is decorated with ornate murals on the interior showing frescoes, statues, ornate furniture, floor to ceiling "windows" looking out on the countryside around Versailles. Only one of the four trains that ran the Versailles route was decorated, so chances weren't great that we would get to ride in it. But I could hope!

And then the train came to the station and we hurried to get on. The first step is very tall and Grandma and her fiancé were having trouble with it. Then of course I had to bring up the stroller, hurrying the whole time because they were making last call and we were still not all on. Traveling with a baby is hard. Traveling with a baby plus a crowd is harder. The car we had chosen was full, so we had to walk through three cars to find seats all together. Then finally we all sat down in a huff, glad to finally be situated.

It took me several minutes to finally notice them. The murals. By sheer luck, we had made it onto the painted train, and surrounding us were frescoed ceilings of angels and saints and kings and queens. There were golden statues in front of floor to ceiling windows standing guard by the doors of the carriage, candles lighting everything up. It was all flat, of course, no real candles and statues and frescoes, but it was still really cool to see them.

When we finally arrived at the station and took the short walk to the palace, the line was already wrapping around in a long S-shaped snake.

"Oh. My. God," Grandma said, stamping her foot a little. "This is riDICulous."

"I'm sure it will go faster than it looks," I told her.

"We have the museum pass. I don't see why we should have to *wait*. You just go stand up there with the baby, Joseph. No one will mind."

"Grandma! I'm not going to cut!"

"I'm just being a bitch and I don't care."

"Grandma!" I laughed. "I can't believe you just said that!"

"Well I am, and I'm tired of standing and this line is ridiculous."

It took an hour, but we finally made it through the line and into the oldest part of the palace.

Versailles was originally a hunting lodge. The Louvre had been the main palace of the king of France. But after Louis XIV was nearly killed in a civil war led by members of the nobility, he fled Paris, traumatized, and resettled in the country. Eventually he would basically hold the entire nobility hostage there "by his invitation" so he could spy on them and ensure there would never be a rebellion again. This strategy didn't end up working out so well for his grandson, Louis XVI, leaving him and his entourage easy picking for the revolution.

Louis XIV often had thousands of nobles living at Versailles or nearby. Versailles was like the dorm of the French nobility. And if you can imagine those nobles having five or so servants to attend them each, the total population, just for the court, was the size of a small city, let alone the soldiers, laborers, and bar maids and other, normal people who lived in Versailles. Much of the time, the grounds of the palace were open to the public, so the peasants and tiny middle class could gawk at the nobility like celebrities as they sauntered around flirting and gossiping all day long.

I wondered why the nobility were so self-absorbed and oblivious to the feelings of the people as the French Revolution stirred around them. I didn't get it until I was at Versailles and realized they were trained to be that way by a megalomaniac suffering from PTSD. Louis XIV was crazy, but he was also a genius, and he was able to successfully hold his kingdom together during a period of huge global change and unrest.

Louis XVI, his grandson, could never have ruled as the Sun King had. He had the power and privilege of a despot, but not the skill for it. He was set up to fail, and when he did, it undid all of France.

After touring the gardens, we did a quick walkthrough of the chateau. The Hall of Mirrors was open after a long restoration, which Talia was excited about since the last time she had been there it was closed. I'm sure it was beautiful, but honestly I don't remember it. The crowd was so large and we were just moving like a sea of people through the house. I forgot all about my dreams of dynasty. If I were able to think as I was pressed by the crowd, I might have reflected that this must have been what the courtiers felt like as they were trapped in their gilded cage by the Sun King. But I couldn't reflect on such grand things in the midst of all those sweaty tourists, and when we came to the end I was exhausted and ready to be home.

Challenge no. 11: Visit

Visit all of the museums in your city (up to five). Museums are how we curate the experience of a community. What can you learn from the experience of *your* community?

12

SONG AND DANCE

Do your best rendition of "Singing in the Rain" in front of the Arc de Triomphe. (Annie C.)

∽

Y ou can blame Grandma for this entire thing. This book. These adventures. All the inspiration and all the suffering I went through.

They all started with Grandma.

Grandma was getting married in Florence. She was eighty-five and she was engaged to a seventy-five-year-old retired prison electrician.

The difference in their age once got me in trouble. For the first six years of their romantic relationship, Grandma didn't tell her boyfriend how old she was, and while he was aware that she was older than him, Grandma kept the fact that she was babysitting when he was baby-sittable a carefully guarded secret.

And who can blame her? As precarious as dating is in your eighties (your nursing home or mine?), why make it

harder by revealing you're a decade older than your significant other?

Unfortunately, I didn't think of the benefits of opacity
when Grandma's boyfriend cornered me at a party a few
years ago.

"So Joe. Tell me," he said, placing his hand encourag-
ingly above my elbow, "how old is your grandmother?"

I normally wouldn't have the faintest idea—birthdays
and ages are not my area—but the heavens must have
wanted to bring some transparency to Grandma's relationship because the answer came to me immediately.

"She's eighty-two."

He nodded, smiled, and said nothing more. It wasn't
until Grandma came up to me red-faced and yelling that I
realized what a victory it was for him.

"Joseph! You told him how old I am?!" she said. "That
was supposed to be a secret!" She was very annoyed.

"Grandma, you've been dating like six years! How have
you not told him?"

"Because it's private. I can't believe you, Joseph," she
growled.

Another time, at my cousin's graduation party, she found
a bottle of Patron and did shots with the twenty-somethings,
then cornered my mother and regaled her with details
about . . . well, I would tell you but my mother said I wasn't
allowed to.

Anyway, after years of "living in sin," Grandma finally
persuaded her boyfriend to make an "honest-enough"
woman out of her, and a year before they had gotten
engaged. I don't know if they ever intended to get married,
but when the prospect of going to Florence came up, we put
a glass of wine in Grandma's hand and tried to convince her
to make it a destination wedding.

"It'll be fun. It doesn't even have to be a real wedding. We'll get a villa and Uncle Steve will get ordained online and marry you himself. It'll be a big party."

Grandma loves a party. She said yes, of course.

Talia found a villa a few miles outside of the city—some Medici's cousin's old place, apparently—that was supposed to be beautiful and drafty and the advertisement said you could see the Duomo from the second floor window. Perfect. We split it forty-three ways with my extended family.

All because my Grandma is always up for a good adventure. I guess I can blame the fact that I was even open to this on her too.

ON OUR LAST day in Paris, we came to the final attraction of our visit. The next day, we would all be leaving France and my adventure would be over.

By that point, I was exhausted. We had been to nine different museums and historical sites. We had eaten at eleven different restaurants and cafés. I had pushed Mars in that stupid shark stroller for miles and miles. I was honestly ready to be done with tourism. I honestly was ready to be done with Paris in general. In my head, I had moved on to Florence. I had pasta and Chianti and David statues on my mind.

But then, just when I thought I had seen all Paris had to offer, there we were in front of the Arc de Triomphe.

It was immense. Beautiful. And also covered in nearly every square inch with memorials to violence.

The Arc de Triomphe is set in the middle of the Champs-Élysées, the busiest, most touristed street in Paris. There, where everyone in France can see it, is not just a beautiful monument, but also as a symbol of Total War, a symbol that was commissioned by Napoleon, built by French Emperors and Kings, paraded in front of by the Germans after the siege of Paris in 1871, then the French after WWI in 1919, then the Nazis in 1941, and then by the Allies in 1944. But what is fascinating about it is that the symbol itself predicted all those future conflicts.

Not long before Napoleon began building the Arc de Triomphe, nearly every war fought in the world followed the philosophy of Elite War, where small armies led by rich nobleman did battle.

France, though, was the first nation to draft its citizens into a single professional military. France was the first national government to say to all of its people, "Oh you're a male between the ages of 18 and 25. One in four of you belong to us." Before that, conscription existed, of course, and people still went to war, obviously, but the French transformed how war was done. Before France, military commanders were chosen by how much money they had or what family they came from. The French chose military leaders based on, you know, how good they were at leading. The same revolutionaries who cut off the head of their king with a guillotine, built a whole new system of warfare.

And the system worked. Despite being in the middle of a revolution that would decimate its nobility, the French defeated half of Europe three different times, so that when Napoleon finally won the Battle of Austerlitz against two of the other biggest European powers, Austria and Russia, France wasn't just the most powerful country in Europe. It was the most powerful country in the world.

It was 1805, and Napoleon decided to build a monument, an arch, one modeled after a similar arch built by Emperor Titus in Rome (which we would be seeing in just a week) to cement not just his personal power, but the legacy of Total

War. Other countries, learning from the French example, rushed to catch up. They dissolved their feudal-style militaries and rebuilt them in the French image. And then a hundred and fifty years, several European wars and two World Wars later, it gave fruit to millions and millions of deaths. All because of an idea.

We looked up at the Arc's immensity, the names of leaders engraved on its sides and the names of the battles on the arch.

We paid our respects to the Tomb of the Unknown Soldier.

And then I had an idea, an idea that wasn't as revolutionary as Total War, but was still pretty exciting.

When I first asked people for adventure suggestions to accomplish in Paris, I got over a hundred ideas for adventures. Some were cool but impractical, others were weird and impossible. There was one adventure I never intended to do, and that was to perform "Singing in the Rain" in the rain under the Arc de Triomphe. Why? So many reasons, but if you've read this far, you probably already know them all by now.

But then, as I was pacing around the monument, watching the cars zoom around the roundabout that had the great Arch in its center, I remembered Grandma.

Grandma was a great dancer. Even more, she *loved* to dance. And she was there, with me, right at that moment.

My mom was also great dancer. She loved to dance, too. And she too was there, with me, right at that moment.

Mars couldn't really dance. He was a baby. But he liked to have fun at least. And if you added me, who did *not* love to dance but would do it for three people I loved, then we would have *four* generations, all dancing together in front of the Arc de Triomphe.

That was an amazing thing.

So I went up to Grandma.

"Grandma, I have an idea," I said. "I want you to perform 'Singing in the Rain' with me."

"What?!" she said. "Are you crazy?!"

"Grandma, it's going to be great. We're going to have four generations. FOUR! Dancing together under the Arc de Triomphe. You're going to love it."

Mom, overhearing the exchange, started singing and dancing.

"I'm siiiinging in the raaaiiin," she sang. She kicked, she spun, she pivoted. It was a simple little dance, but it looked great.

"I loved singing this growing up," she said. "I loved Fred Astaire. I wanted to marry him. I was so upset when I found out he was already married."

Grandma got in line. She kicked. She spun. She pivoted.

"Just siiiinging in the rain!" they sang.

I jumped in, didn't even think, didn't even care that half of Paris was out on the Champs-Élysées and I was making a fool out of myself. I just kicked. I spun. I pivoted.

I danced.

Was I growing right now? Was I in the process of learning an important life lesson? Or was it just that I was with the right group of people, my crazy Grandma and my fun-loving mom and my toddler son who loved me best when I was making silly faces at him?

Either way, it was working. Maybe adventures are only as good as the people you're doing them with.

"What a wonderful feeling," we sang, "I'm happy again."

Talia handed me Mars, who could not dance, but smiled and laughed, and we were all dancing together.

"Just singing in the rain. Just singing in the rain. Just singing. In. The rain."

We danced like that for a few minutes, until we had gone through all the words we knew, or that my mom knew, really. And then we laughed, so much laughing.

We gave a bow. We had gathered a small crowd by that point. I think someone threw us a few coins, even.

While we hugged and then gathered our things to get ready to go, I thought again about the power of legacy. I had been thinking a lot about legacy since Versailles. Louis XIV was the pinnacle of a dynasty, a family who shaped France, who shaped the world. As I had walked through the gardens of Versailles, I could feel Louis' ambition in that place. I could see how he wanted to create a kingdom that wouldn't just last his lifetime, but that would last for a thousand years. And yet after he was gone his dynasty was wiped out in less than a hundred.

As I walked, I thought about what kind of legacy I would pass to Mars, whose head was laying on my chest in his baby carrier. I wondered whether it would be a palace or power or wealth or a family name that would be remembered. A book is one way to leave a legacy, but a child is a much better way. Maybe I would never be able to give him money or power, but I could give him a few ideas, ideas about the right way to live that could provide for his family but also give him happiness that could spread to the people he loved. I had wanted to give him something he could touch, hold, taste and see that it was good, but no, the best legacy I could leave him were my ideas about the right way to live.

And as we turned our backs on that monument to an idea about war, I made a vow to Mars to pass down a set of ideas that would bring him peace and love and life.

But there was one more adventure to do, the biggest, scariest, hardest adventure of all. I was about to meet Gilles.

Challenge no. 12: Dance

Perform a song and dance with your family or friends.

Choose a song. Quickly choreograph a dance. Then go outside to a busy street (or inside to a public space like a mall) and perform your best number! How does it feel? Terrifying? Exhilarating? Humiliating? Empowering? A little bit of all four of those?

CATACOMBS

CATACOMBS REDUX: Explore the huge system of caverns, caves, and catacombs below Paris, left from when the Romans quarried the region for stone. Every once in a while a bit of Paris plunges into a hole (more information from National Geographic). (Suggested by Dan K.)

~

I t was our last night in Paris, and we were back at Spring, this time with Grandma, the fiancé, and my parents. We had found a babysitter through an expat friend, and my dad had just bought $300 of wine from the sommelier.

"Don't forget about the conversion rate, Dad," I said.

"It's fine. We're celebrating!" Later, when he got the bill, he would whine and complain, but just then I let him enjoy himself. The menu was different than when we had been there the first time, but still amazing. Afterward, Dad told me it was the best meal he'd ever had. Even Grandma loved it.

But before dinner was over I had to leave. With a not-quite-full-enough stomach I stood up and excused myself.

"Good luck, Joe!" said Dad.

"You're going to do great," said Talia.

"Where's he going?" said Grandma.

"To see the catacombs underneath Paris," Mom explained.

"The catacombs?! What in the world?"

I let them explain, kissed my wife, and walked up the stairs and out into the night.

I was late to meet Gilles.

The day after Albert had given me his contact information, I emailed Gilles, who was perhaps the top world expert on the caves and catacombs of Paris. He had written three books on the subject, had been featured in the National Geographic, NPR, the New York Times, the Wall Street Journal, and Pixar (next time you watch *Ratatouille* look for his name in the credits). I honestly didn't expect him to reply the first time, that I would have to follow up again and again. But in just a few minutes, he did respond.

"I will take you," he said, but first, there was an exhibit about the caves of Paris he was seeing with a friend nearby. "Will you come?"

"Yes, of course," I replied.

And so I had met Gilles just across the Saint-Sulpice Square at the 6th Arrondissement's city hall, a large, official-looking building with columns and a huge staircase. The whole deal. Gilles was with a quiet, older woman who spoke only French, and we walked through the exhibit.

My first impression of Gilles was of a lovable nerd. The exhibit was mostly just photos and text with a few old books behind glass cases. It was all in French, but Gilles translated for me, telling me about Charles-Axel Guillaumot who worked to restore the catacombs after they began collapsing in the eighteenth century.

You can imagine if you were walking along in your city and suddenly heard a giant rumbling and then a long crashing sound as loud as anything you'd ever heard in your life, then a plume of dust go up as you watched a portion of your city, perhaps an office building or a row of houses or a church, disappear into the ground. You would cry out and approach the collapse, and, if you were very brave, tentatively inch up to the edge, only to see darkness and a cone-shaped pit far as the eye could see.

People went hysterical, blaming devils and God's judgment on the wicked, but of course, it all came back to the French's insatiable need to construct beautiful buildings. From the Romans to the first French kings all the way until the eighteenth century, people had been mining limestone out of the banks of the Seine. This limestone had been used to build the great chateaus, cathedrals, and monuments of Paris, including Notre Dame, the Louvre, Luxembourg Palace, and so many others, all with that traditional Parisian hue.

Unfortunately for the residents of Rue d'Enfer, and all the others who were killed by the collapses over the centuries, some of the miners were not as forward thinking as they should have been, and used an illegal technique to dig straight down and then go along a seam of stone horizontally, sometimes sixty feet or more underground, until it ran out. Then they would abandon the mine, cover up the hole, and leave the problem to someone else. Over a thousand years, this began to become a major issue as the ceilings of these man-made caves began to slowly disintegrate. Eventually the ground above became unstable enough for catastrophe to strike. Dozens of people were swallowed up at a time.

Louis XVI, then a young king, appointed Charles-Axel Guillaumot, a hotshot engineer, trained in Italy, to set about mapping, clearing, and fortifying the caves of Paris. The network of bad mines was so extensive, and the threat of cave-ins such a problem, that it is not hyperbole to say Guillaumot saved Paris.

Much of Gilles' work of the last three decades has been documenting Guillamot's contributions to Paris, and three books into it, they're extensive.

After touring the exhibit with Gilles for an hour, I went back home, but before I left, he agreed to take me through the catacombs, and promised to set a date over email.

I couldn't believe it, honestly. After the first cataphile had flaked out, I had almost given up hope to see the real catacombs of Paris. Then, by sheer luck, I had mentioned my challenge to Albert at the writer's group in Au Chat Noir and he had told me about Gilles. And now here I was, planning to meet him in just a few days to finally explore the catacombs.

But when I emailed Gilles, he told me he was out of town for a week, exploring some caves outside of Paris. He wouldn't get back until my family was in town. I worried it was never going to happen.

But I also knew that somehow I had to get into the catacombs or this whole adventure would be ruined. My trip to Paris, my book, all these adventures, they hung on the whim of a cataphile, and my experience with cataphiles so far was that they were pretty flakey.

If I had learned one thing from this trip, it was this: If you want to have a great adventure, you have to be relentless.

So I had emailed him.

I emailed him every day.

Then I texted him.

He didn't respond at first. I kept at it.

Then, just a few days before we were set to leave, he emailed back.

"I just arrived back in town," he had said. "We will go Thursday night. Meet me near Luxembourg Gardens at 10:30 p.m. Bring rubber boots and a flashlight." Signed, "Gilles."

Thursday would be my last night in Paris. We had already made reservations at Spring. If I went to the catacombs, I would be cutting short our best, and last, dinner in Paris. I would be down below Paris until early in the morning. I would get only a few hours of sleep, since I had to get up the next day to catch the flight to Italy.

If I went, I would be putting myself in the hands of someone who I'd only met for a few moments, someone who was drawn to dark places and secret societies. I would be following this stranger into the darkness, into caverns with water up to your knees, through tunnels where if I got lost, I would never be able to find my way back, to a place where, if he left me, or worse attacked me, no one would find me again, maybe ever.

I didn't think twice.

"I'll be there," I said.

I was finally going to the catacombs.

As I HURRIED AWAY from Spring along Rue Bailleul, late to meet Gilles, I realized I didn't have time to take the metro. A cab would take forever to find, plus I didn't have the money. The only thing to do was run. So I did. I ran across Pont du

Carrousel up along the Seine then down Rue Bonaparte to get to our flat so I could change out of my restaurant clothes and into my cataphile outfit. It took me way too long. I knew I would never make it in time.

When I made it up the stairs and rushed into the flat I was completely out of breath. The babysitter was still there.

"Talia will be along in a little while," I told her. "I'm just changing and running back out."

I'm sure she thought I was crazy, but I didn't have time to worry about it. I changed into track pants and put on my sneakers. I put on a light windbreaker. Then I grabbed my bag with my notebook in it. I wasn't sure I would be able to write in the dark, but I would be upset if I didn't have it. Last I grabbed the smallest flashlight in the world, and then headed back out.

"Have a great night!" I said to the babysitter. I didn't hear her respond as I ran back down the stairs.

The flashlight I should explain. After our first meeting, Gilles instructed me to get two things: boots, because we would be walking through water up to our knees in some places, and a flashlight. Not expecting to be spelunking when I packed for Paris months before, I had of course brought neither. And so I looked for an outdoor store, and the day after I met Gilles, I went there.

The outdoor store was a bit confusing. Real estate as it is in Paris, the company couldn't find one big building all together, and so they had rented smaller storefronts over two city blocks. Then they just broke up a regular sports store into departments and scattered them throughout their twenty-seven locations. It was impossible to find anything. I went into the snowboarding shop first, but quickly realized I wouldn't find what I needed. Then I found a water sport store which had surfboards and water skis but no boots.

I finally found the shoe store after much confused walking between buildings. Good news: they had boots! Bad news, they were ninety-five euro. *Merde*, that was a lot of money for rubber boots I would never wear that also would never fit in my suitcase to take home. I decided instead to buy a pair of breathable, quick-dry running shoes instead, but as I looked at their selection, I realized their cheapest pair was *more* expensive than the boots. I bought the shoes and then left the store in disgust to find a flashlight.

It took me three more wrong stores to find the one that stocked flashlights. The prices were just as bad for flashlights as they were for shoes. The normal, small LED flashlight was thirty-five euro. I did have a few good flashlights in the States, so this wasn't exactly a long-term investment. I finally opted for the cheapest flashlight they had, a single LED bulb on the tiniest of keychains that was advertised as the smallest flashlight in the world. It was about fifteen dollars. Not great, but not as bad as the thirty-five euro one.

Visiting the catacombs was turning out to be expensive.

It was this flashlight I grabbed on my rush out the door. There was no on/off switch and no button. You turned it on by screwing the bottom a little tighter. Turning it off was more precarious, since if you screwed it too far the itty-bitty batteries would fall out.

And this very thing did in fact happen. I was so late to meet Gilles that I was sprinting to our meeting spot not far from the Luxembourg gardens. I slowed down to catch my breath, and took out my flashlight to make sure it was working. It was—great!—but when I twisted it to turn it off the back fell off and the one of the batteries popped out and scattered on the pavers and into the dark Parisian night. It was 10:35, and I was supposed to meet Gilles at 10:30.

"No!" I shouted. "This can't be happening right now."

The street was almost empty but I still felt like someone having a breakdown as I got down on my hands and knees to look for the missing battery.

I thought about abandoning the battery and risking the catacombs sans-flashlight. I had a vision of getting lost in the pitch black like Jean Valjean. Right about the time I was going to leave, I saw something shiny in the crack of a paver. It was the battery. I put it back in the flashlight and twisted it tight, vowing to leave it on for the rest of the night.

At 10:45, I saw Gilles waiting for me. He looked like a painter in a pair of filthy blue overalls. He was standing by a bus stop when I approached. "Hi, Gilles. I'm so sorry I'm late."

"I told you to bring boots."

"My shoes dry quickly," I said.

"Ok."

Then, without another word, he opened the grate with a hook and said, "Quick, go," and I climbed down into the deep.

I WASN'T PREPARED. I didn't have my flashlight out, and even so I would have been afraid of dropping it while climbing. I had no idea how far the ladder went. I was still huffing after running. The whole situation drowned me in adrenaline. Was I really doing this right now?

I expected the climb to last for a long time. The catacombs are twenty meters down, about sixty feet. After a few seconds of climbing I worried that my arms, tired after running, wouldn't be able to hold me up and that I would fall the rest of the way.

But I needn't have worried. The ladder ended after only

a few more feet on a dusty cement floor and I waited for Gilles to cover the hatch and come down himself.

When he got to the bottom, his flashlight lit up our surroundings. I saw that we were in a service tunnel, with pipes and wires strung up along the wall. There was graffiti everywhere.

When Gilles reached the bottom, he took off down the tunnel. I scrambled to pull out my flashlight, which was still on, and follow him.

The tunnel was long, too far for me to see with my tiny flashlight. It had a series of climbs and dips. You went up a short set of stairs and then it would be flat for twenty feet and then you went down again. At the top of each flight was a little gate, about hip high. When we got to the first one, Gilles opened it, and then as I passed through, he pointed to it, indicating I should close it. We went like this for a long time. Down the stairs. Up a flight. Open the gate. Close the gate.

I was underground. I was in the catacombs. I was thrilled! And yet, this didn't feel like the catacombs I was expecting.

But then, Gilles turned down a corridor which went into a long staircase. When we got to the bottom there was a concrete wall. We had reached a dead end.

"Okay, you will go first?" It was the first thing he had said to me since we got underground.

"Where do I go?" I said, looking at the wall blocking our way.

He pointed to a small hole carved beside the wall.

To be clear, I'm not great in cramped spaces. I abhor going in the crawlspace under my house. I had a nightmare a few nights before I met Gilles about crawling into a tight tunnel, just like the one I was looking at. In the dream, I got jammed so tight that they had to break my hip bone to get me out.

You might be thinking, "Um, maybe you're not the best person to go into the catacombs then."

And I would say, "Yes! You're probably right. And yet here we are!"

But Gilles was looking at me and from the way he had been speeding through the tunnels earlier, it seemed he was in a hurry.

Well, this is what I signed up for. I thought.

I took off my bag, tossed it into the hole, and climbed in headfirst.

The little tunnel was about a body length long and just wide enough to fit a large man. It curved around the concrete wall, the wall presumably built by the underground police, that had been blocking our way. I shimmied through slowly. The hardest part was getting out gracefully, since you emerged head first. My technique was to stick my arm out and kind of crab walk out of the hole. I was dirty, but all in all the experience wasn't as terrifying as I feared. Not sure I wanted to do it again, though.

Of course, after Gilles got through and we walked a few more minutes, we came to a second wall and a tunnel just big enough to die in.

This time Gilles went first. I repeated the steps from before, tossed my bag through first, shimmied in, crab walk out, but this time Gilles snapped a picture of me with a little digital camera as I was in what I'm sure was the most embarrassing pose of my life. Thanks Gilles.

Once we got through this tunnel he seemed to relax. When I first met Gilles, he told me the story of how he first experienced the catacombs. He said it was like being born a second time. I could tell we had officially made it into the catacombs. Gilles was home.

He started talking to me then. He told me where we were under the city. We came to an inscription in the wall.

"1780 * 80 G," it said, in an old fashioned script.

"1780 for the year this tunnel was built. 80 is the section of the catacombs. G is for Guilleumot, who was inspector during this part of the construction."

We walked on. It wasn't cold here like I was expecting. It was perfectly temperate. I took off my jacket and tied it around my waist. The floor of the tunnel was soft, packed down dirt. It smelled like dust and nothingness.

I realized I had made it. The tunnel above was just the foyer. These were the real catacombs. And here I was, sixty feet underground, with one of the top cataphiles in Paris! My last night in Paris and this was the celebration. I couldn't believe I had actually made it. I walked behind Gilles beaming, tears coming to my eyes. I was so happy.

We kept walking and the tunnel sloped down a bit and the ground was covered in a pool of clear water. When we walked through the silt swirled up and muddied the water. My shoes were wet now, but I didn't mind. I was just doing my best to keep up with Gilles. Then we walked through another pool, this one a little deeper. We walked through it without pausing and when we came out, my pants were wet to the ankle and my shoes were squeaking.

We went through many pools during the course of our time in the catacombs. Some up to our knees, but most to our ankles. One was so deep we had to put our feet on the bricks along the sides of the cave and walk balancing between the walls.

We had only been in the catacombs for fifteen minutes, but

it already felt like hours. The novelty of the darkness was already beginning to wear off. I don't want to sound whiny, but my legs were wet, my shoes were squeaky, my clothes were dirty, and it was quite late. I tried to banish thoughts about how long we would be down here and remind myself how hard I had worked to get this amazing experience and how lucky I was.

That's when we came around a corner to see a giant tombstone.

In the late 1790s, right in the middle of the French Revolution's Reign of Terror, a middle aged man named Philibert Aspairt went missing after his shift guarding a hospital that served revolutionaries. He wasn't seen again for over a decade. It wasn't until eleven years later, after the inspector was back at work post-Revolution once again reinforcing the collapsing tunnels, that Aspairt's body was found. "Body" was probably too generous. By then it was just his bones and some dried skin.

To this day, no one knows why he wandered into the tunnels or why he never left them. Perhaps it was the sight of so many bloodied revolutionaries coming through the hospital doors, which he stood guard over, or perhaps a desire to escape the constant scrutiny. During the revolution, if you weren't seen as nationalist enough you could be sent to the guillotine with no trial. Perhaps he simply wanted to escape the pressure cooker that was Paris in 1793, if only for a little while.

Whatever it was, one night Aspairt went down a stairway in the hospital courtyard into the catacombs. People didn't ask questions when individuals disappeared, and no search was made for him. But when they found him, instead of carting his body back to the surface, they decided to bury him where he lay. Later, a surprisingly large and ornate tomb was built over his grave.

And standing in front of the tomb, while Gilles snapped my picture, I couldn't help but think for a relatively unimportant person, he certainly got a really nice grave.

We walked on. One odd thing about the catacombs is that limestone is like an acoustic sponge. I expected there to be echoes through the catacombs, that we would be able to hear everything that was happening within a kilometer of us, transformed by a million refractions. Instead, you heard nothing, barely even your own breathing. There was no smell or temperature there. And so the combined effect was sensory deprivation. You began to feel like you were in your own head, not in any real existence. It was a safe, womb-like feeling. I was starting to understand why Gilles felt like going to the catacombs was his rebirth.

After about a mile of walking we came into a much more modern section. Carved limestone walls were replaced by brick and concrete. There were steel doors and graffitti on all the walls. Most notably, there were color coded arrows painted on the walls with German words written above them.

We had reached the Nazi bunkers.

There are three bunkers used by the Nazis in the catacomb network, Gilles told me. This one was built underneath a French high school by a French businessman who was trying to earn favor with the German military. He spent a lot of money to build it, but by the time it was finished, the Germans had already fled the city from the Allied army.

I forgot to ask what happened to that French businessman who worked for the Nazis when the Allies recaptured Paris.

We walked around the bunker, peeking into its rooms. There were old bathrooms, some larger spaces, but most of it was just hallways with walls covered in graffiti.

I felt fairly safe in the catacombs. The limestone walls had a kind of cocoon-like feel to them. But those bunkers made me uneasy. I found myself constantly looking around corners, expecting someone to dart out. When Gilles said it was time to continue, I wasn't sad to leave.

"I read that the police discovered a movie theater down here," I said as we walked. "Have you been there?"

"Many of the police are cataphiles. There was a group who did that."

"They said there were symbols painted in the cave. They thought maybe it was a secret society."

"Not a secret society. Just cataphile. People who love the catacombs."

"So you know who they are?"

"Of course," he said.

We came to a long section of straight tunnels that seemed like they were built under a boulevard. Many of the tunnels had names on them for the streets under which they were built. Of course, those were the street names in the 18th and 19th centuries, so many have changed, but this one seemed to be under a main boulevard that was still in existence. There were two parallel tunnels, one for each side of the boulevard, presumably because having one larger tunnel would take too much reinforcement.

We walked for about thirty minutes. There were several turns, several more pools of water to walk through. Eventually we came to a section made out of stone bricks. We made a few turns and walked up some steps. There was an old well, covered up. When we turned again the short hall ended abruptly, cemented off.

In a shallow pit next to us was a pile of bones.

"This is the ossuary," said Gilles. "You've been to the ossuary, yes, with the bones?"

"Yes, I went soon after I arrived in Paris."

"We are at the edge of the ossuary."

Gilles told me that he had once been in this section when he came across a group of young people from Norway. They had been in the catacombs for three days. That night they were sleeping right there, close to the ossuary. They were lost, he told me, and he helped them find where they needed to go.

"They weren't scared to sleep next to the bones?" I asked him.

"No, why not? They are nothing."

I couldn't imagine spending three days here. I couldn't imagine *sleeping* there, especially if I didn't know where I was. It sounded like a nightmare. I began to get a little sick just thinking about it.

We backtracked a bit, and then, as we were walking, I began to hear voices. I felt a knot tighten in my stomach. I hoped he would stop, let them go by, but I knew he wouldn't. I saw two lights and then they were calling for us and he was talking back, all in French of course. We got closer and I saw they were two men, one a bit older than the other. They spoke rapid French to Gilles, who didn't introduce me. I thought they were probably friends. The cataphile community is small. They must know each other.

They talked for a long time, and I tried to smile, to look interested, like I understood a little even though I didn't. At last they turned to me and Gilles said something about me in French. He was pointing at my flashlight, speaking quickly. The cataphiles laughed. I knew they were laughing at me, and I began to feel shame start down my spine. One motioned to the flashlight, and so I held it up, smiling.

"The smallest flashlight in the world," I said. It *was* kind of funny.

They probably didn't understand and they continued in French. Gilles spoke and did I hear scorn in his voice? I felt like such a novice, so unprepared, which I was of course. It was embarrassing.

After ten minutes of talking we continued on our way. We walked for a while in silence. I wondered if Gilles was mad at me.

"Those cataphiles were talking about a spot," he said finally. "I want to go look. Maybe a collapse."

"Ok," I said. A collapse sounded kind of serious. "Is the tunnel okay? Structurally."

"Yes, but I want to make sure."

So we walked for ten minutes or so in the direction the two cataphiles had come from. We turned twice, I wasn't keeping track of which direction, and then came to it. It was a wider, taller tunnel than the others, and it stretched off in another direction a long ways from where the hole in the wall was.

"You stay here," he said. "I'm going to look."

"Ok."

I watched him as he crawled into the hole on his hands and knees and then as his light disappeared a little. I could mostly still see him, the light of his flashlight off into the distance. And then he was gone.

I was left there alone. Gilles' flashlight had provided plenty of light for the both of us. Now that he was gone, I realized my flashlight only extended five or so feet in front of me. Beyond that it was all darkness. I realized without him, I would be all but blind and utterly lost.

At first I was excited he was gone because I had been wanting to try something. I lifted the light and carefully twisted it until the darkness covered me. This is what I wanted to feel, what the darkness felt like.

One of my first observations was just how dark it was. It was impossibly dark. Unless you're in a cave right now, you can't imagine how dark the catacombs are. Even if you *have* been in one, as soon as you leave and you're back in the light it's impossible to remember darkness as it really is. Even now, as I think back to the catacombs, I know that my memories are too bright, a manufactured fantasy rather than reality. Our brains are made for light. Darkness fails to compute.

I tried to listen, but heard nothing. I tried to see, even though the light was off, to spot anything, but there was nothing to see. I felt for the wall behind me, which was cold and soft to the touch.

I couldn't help it. In the midst of that impossible darkness, I started to worry.

What if Gilles is screwing with me? I thought.

He had been so chummy with those cataphiles. What if he wanted to leave me out here for a while, make me sweat because of my too small flashlight? What if this was the way they hazed Americans?

I didn't really know Gilles. Yes, I had met him briefly. Yes, he had given tours to NPR and National Geographic. But maybe he was only nice to people he had something to gain from and he had realized I couldn't give him very much. He had barely said ten words to me since we had come down into the catacombs. Was I sitting here in the darkness while he was going another route to abandon me? What did I know about him? Nothing. I knew nothing about him.

The dark began to torment me. I thought about how Philibert Aspairt felt down here. I turned on my flashlight, but it just made it worse because I was reminded of how dependent I was on Gilles in that moment. I was in a network of caves that spanned over a hundred miles, where I had no sense of direction, no map, no idea where the exits were in case I wanted to leave, and my only source of light was literally (and I use that word very carefully) the smallest flashlight in the world.

If Gilles did leave me, I thought, trying to keep my cool, *what would I do?*

I looked back the way I came. My light didn't shine that far back so all I really saw was a ring of darkness.

I knew there were two parallel tunnels that led underneath the Luxembourg Gardens, where I had first entered. I had been going too fast, though. There were too many turns, too many tunnels half-filled with water. There was no way I would be able to get back there.

I knew there were other exits. We had passed a few ladders going up through the ceiling. If I could somehow trace my way back there, it might lead to a manhole cover on the streets above. I could walk back and try to find it. I could climb the ladder sixty feet up. As tired as I was, and as worn out from sprinting here earlier, I knew I could climb to the top. But I also knew how pointless it would be. All the entrances to the catacombs were welded shut, and that meant almost every *exit* was welded shut too, all but the one I had come through, which I would likely never be able to find again.

How long could I last, then, hanging from the top, banging against the door at two in the morning, just hoping someone would hear me and break it open?

I knew I could have found my way out of there if I knew the streets. With the tunnels all labelled, I knew that if you recognized the streets, you could find your way through the tunnels. But even after living there for most of the spring, I had no faith in my ability to navigate on street names alone.

I had gotten lost dozens of times in Paris *aboveground*. I couldn't imagine trying to find my way down here with my worthless flashlight.

I was in a tomb. These caves were named after the bones of Paris's dead. I looked out into the darkness but there was nothing to see.

My only thought was that I was going to die here, hours before I was set to leave Paris.

All for a stupid book.

As terrifying as it was to consider the idea that Gilles had ditched me in some twisted cataphile hazing, it was just as bad to crawl in after him. If it *was* a collapse, like Gilles had told me, there was a good chance it wasn't stable, especially if I went bumbling through it.

Plus, he told me to stay there. If he *was* in there, and *hadn't* abandoned me to die alone and terrified, then what would I say to him? How humiliating to go in and admit that I couldn't hack it, that I was actually *scared* of the place he considered the site of his second birth.

I waited like that, getting more and more anxious about the possibilities, for five minutes. Then ten. Then fifteen. Still Gilles didn't come back.

Fifteen minutes underground feels like a lifetime. And I had been living a lifetime in growing panic.

I finally decided. Forget humiliation. I was going to find out for myself if Gilles, the famed cataphile, really did abandon me.

I climbed into the hole.

It wasn't an easy climb. The first part I could go on my hands and knees, but then I had to crawl on my belly for a few body lengths, listening all the while for sounds of the dirt shifting above me. Fortunately, the tunnel held and then the cave opened up and I was able to walk at a crouch.

I went around a corner and saw the light of Gilles' flashlight. All the tightness in my chest went away.

I came around the bend to see him crouched in what I can only describe as a big hole filled with dirt. He looked up at me.

"I came to find you," I said.

"You were a little afraid?" he asked calmly.

I paused. "A little."

"You have nothing to fear down here." He said it so gently, like a kind grandfather.

He looked at the hole for a few more minutes. It didn't seem to be collapsing but was surprisingly large.

Then he turned and walked past me back into the mouth of the cave. I followed him, crawling back out, back along the tunnel where we had come.

"We will get to a part where there is some crouching," he said as we walked. "It is a hard section. Is that okay?"

"Sure. That's fine."

"There is another way, but sometimes it is flooded up to your waist. I do not think that would be good for us tonight."

"Okay." I didn't care which way we went. I was just happy we were talking about the exit.

We walked on. Eventually we reached a place where the walls widened into a large room.

"The beach," he said. There was graffiti there but also murals: a large one of a wave and some mountains, an amazing replica of the Mona Lisa, a very good, classic nude, a Japanese woman wearing a hat. And then cruder art: yellow mushrooms weaving up the wall, the eye of Ra.

In the middle of a room was a sculpture of a bull standing up that was made out of chicken wire and mud. Its arms were stretched out to the side and they held charred reeds for torches. The room smelled like smoke and musk.

"People have parties here sometimes," said Giles.

We kept walking. It was a long walk, the longest of the night. I was exhausted. I had been ready to be done two hours before. I knew it was at least one in the morning. Maybe later. We kept walking.

"That's the way with the water," he said, pointing to a tunnel off to the left. Sure enough, there was a long pool of water.

Not long after we came to the hard part, a crouching section that made the quads burn while you walked through. Giles didn't slow though, and so I didn't either. The ceiling raised for a moment, but then we were crouching again, lower this time. This happened again, the ceiling raised and you got some relief and then we would crouch, lower than ever. My legs were on fire. I felt a knot wrenching up my back. I began to long for the night sky. It went on for ten minutes.

Eventually the tunnel got so low we had to crawl on our hands and knees, then our bellies.

But then finally we were in a wider tunnel, no longer the catacombs, some in-between place. We climbed for a while, then came to a hole in the ceiling. Gilles went first, pressing himself up and slithering through. Then it was my turn. I felt the top of the hole press against my shoulders, felt my hips sliding through.

And then I was out.

In a different tunnel, but this one in the open air. There was light in the distance; moonlight, but still it was the brightest thing I had seen in hours.

I checked my watch. It was two in the morning. I had been in the catacombs for over three hours. And I wasn't home yet.

We walked along the tunnel for almost a kilometer. I

realized we were in an old abandoned train track station. Finally we got to the end of the tunnel and were out in the open, walking along the tracks. There were plants everywhere, the smell of grass and night and spring. It was cold outside, but I didn't put on my jacket. The open air felt amazing.

We walked silently, and I felt an extreme warmth of gratefulness to Gilles. He had spent so much time showing me his passion, the catacombs, something so few people get to see. I suddenly wanted everyone to know about this, to allow them to experience the same thing. But walking through the abandoned tracks I realized how few would actually get to see what I'd seen.

"How many cataphiles are there?" I had asked Gilles earlier, when we were still the caves.

"A few hundred," he said.

So few, and yet there was so much to explore. Eventually, we climbed up the wall and over a fence to get back out on the street. A short walk later and Gilles was saying he was at his apartment.

"Goodnight," he said simply.

"Thank you so much. This was amazing. Thank you," I said.

He gave me a small wave, and then was gone.

It took me thirty minutes more to get back to my house. I almost got lost, but soon found the edge of Luxembourg Gardens and made my way back to Rue des Canettes, up the stairs, and into my flat.

The babysitter was gone of course, and Talia was asleep on the pull-out. I heard my father snoring in the other room.

I peeled off my clothes, which were caked in silt, and took a shower as quietly as I could, watching the pale sediment fall off me and float down the drain, back into the deep.

~

Challenge no. 13: Illegal

Late at night or early morning, go somewhere *slightly* illegal. Walk in the middle of the road, visit a closed park, find your way into a construction site. How does it feel to transgress just a little bit?

EPILOGUE: HOME

We got up late for the first time since we had arrived in Paris. My parents were on an earlier flight and had agreed to take Mars with them. We picked up the house, so silent without our toddler, then locked up, and left for the last time. We went to Gérard Mulot for a final croissant. And then we took the metro to a bus station in a part of Paris we didn't recognize.

We waited a while for the bus, and when it finally came, it took us through the edge of the city, past La Défense, and then out of Paris, into the country hills beyond.

Talia fell asleep.

I saw fields of yellow flowers so bright they hurt your eyes. I saw the shreds of small towns. I slept.

As I slept, my mind came back to this one moment two weeks before. It was right after I had performed at Au Chat Noir, and I had walked out of that restaurant exhilarated, only to realize three things, nearly simultaneously: 1) my outdated phone was at eleven percent battery, 2) I had no cash, and 3) the metro in Paris closed at one a.m., which was five minutes ago. I had no idea how would I get home.

After panicking for a few moments, I started to think about my options. I could go by foot. I figured it was about three miles back. I might be able to walk that in an hour, but if I got lost (and let's be honest, I was going to get lost), the Paris street map in my phone would be utterly useless when my phone died in about fifteen minutes.

"Wow, Joe. Good work. Real great," I mumbled to myself.

All the triumph I had been feeling from my performance had slipped off of me like shoes that didn't quite fit. I was alone, I was cold, and I was getting more and more anxious.

I thought about turning back to Au Chat Noir and asking Albert for a ride, or more embarrassingly, a loan for a cab, but that would be a severe violation of my deeply held rule to never ask for help ever, ever, ever.

I've got this, I thought. *I can figure this out.*

So with grim determination, I turned on my phone and while I walked in the direction I hoped would lead me home, I started to memorize as much of the map as I could. My plan was to keep my phone off as much as possible, and then turn it back on only when I got lost. It was a stupid plan, but it was the best one I had.

I was about five blocks from Chat Noir when I saw a group of drunk men arguing by a street corner. I watched them carefully, my fingers reaching to my keys which I might be able to use as a weapon in case something happened. Getting mugged would turn this into a much different kind of adventure. It was one in the morning, one-thirty now, and while Paris is fairly safe for the most part, it does have a reputation for muggings and even stabbings if you're in the wrong place at the wrong time. It was officially the wrong time.

But then I saw something.

Behind the arguing drunk guys was a long row of bikes. Not just any bikes, but the Vélib bikes.

The best way to see any city is on bike. There's something about being street level, on the road but not cooped up in a car, able to look all around you but faster and more free than if you were walking. About two weeks after arriving in Paris, I had gotten up the nerve to try out the Vélib bikes that were stationed all over the city. Vélibs were government-run rent-a-bikes. You put your card into the payment kiosk, take your bike out of its stand, ride to your destination, and then park it at another stand nearby, all for less than a metro ticket.

I had explored a lot of Paris by Vélib, had ridden to the opera house, the Louvre, the Apple store. I had biked to Coutume instead of walking a few times and had ridden up and down the Quai de Seine. Navigating Paris' traffic, the boulevards and avenues and rues, was very exciting (although Talia would never go with me because the cars and the traffic rules stressed her out).

And standing across the street from that group of argumentative drunk guys, I realized a bike was the perfect way to get home.

Crossing the street, I walked over to the Vélib station and paid for a bike. My hands were shaking because of the cold and the excitement of it, and so it took a while. I hoped the guys on the corner wouldn't notice me. My cheeks felt hot, even though it was so cold out. I took a last look at the map on my phone and turned it off.

Then I got on my bike and started pedaling down the dark streets of Paris.

I had planned out a route to take me southwest toward the Seine. If I went straight west, I could miss my turn to get down to Saint Germain. I could have gone straight south and just waited until I found the Seine. From the Seine I could easily find my way home, but the Seine is the shape of a rainbow, and it was at its farthest point from where I was. It was now 1:35 a.m. If Talia wasn't asleep, she must be wondering where I was by that point. Going southwest, I could get to the Seine quickly and, hopefully, not get lost from there.

With my perfect plan in mind, I set off down Rue Oberkampf, a brightly lit street empty of cars and people. It was an easy ride. The streets were level, even a little downhill, sloping toward the river. I pedaled slow, careful not to burn my energy. I stopped at a red light, then signalled when it turned green, though there was no one to signal to, and turned left down Rue de Nemours.

But I had turned one street too early. It ended on a dead end. I turned around and went back the way I came, but then went the wrong way again and found myself on a whole new road.

Just a few minutes in and I was lost.

We're not lost, Joe. This is fine. We've got this.

Now the road was uphill, and the buildings beside the narrow streets more dilapidated. A bald man in a dark coat eyed me and I pedaled a bit faster. When I saw Boulevard Voltaire, a wide road that cut through much of Paris, I thought I remembered it from my map. So I turned left down the boulevard and let it take me miles the wrong way.

The route I had chosen was supposed to take me past the old Bastille. Then I would follow the roundabout to Boulevard Henri IV and cross the Seine at the tip of Île Saint-Louis (a small island in the Seine in the middle of Paris that's covered in Berthillon ice cream shops).

And so when I got to a giant roundabout after about ten minutes of cycling, I figured it was Place de la Bastille. I didn't see any signs saying Bastille, though, which I thought was odd, but it was still a roundabout and I was looking for a roundabout. Of course, I had never been to the Bastille. If I had, I would have known there was a tall column in the center of the roundabout, the July Column, and it looked nothing like the roundabout I was now looking at.

But I didn't know that, so I began riding around the circle. "Henri IV, Henri IV, Henri IV," I said to myself looking for my route. There were ten streets and boulevards that shot off of that roundabout, and it was so big it took several minutes to pedal around the whole thing. But when I got all the way back to the street I had started on without seeing Henri IV, I stopped and cursed. *Merde.*

What had happened? Where had I gone wrong? It was 2:01 a.m. now. I felt like I was in some far-flung corner of urban Paris. It might still be hours until I would get home; that is, if I could ever find the correct route.

And so I took out my phone and pressed the power button.

Nothing. I tried again. Still nothing. My phone wouldn't turn on.

Merde. Merde. Merde.

I was in a part of town I didn't recognize, on this stupid roundabout with a dozen different roads going to it, most of which would probably lead me to all the wrong places, and with a dead phone I had no way of figuring out the right ones from the wrong ones. It was insanely late. And I know I've said this, but it was *cold*. Ughhh, all I wanted was for this night to end.

But what if it never ended? What if I never found my way home? What if I kept biking, kept circling the city, never seeing anything I recognized, just getting farther and farther from the center of the city? I imagined myself collapsing on a patch of damp grass off to the side of the road somewhere and shivering myself to sleep until the sun rose.

And then a peace fell over me. The sun would be up in a few hours. I could circle Paris, getting more and more lost for hours, but before too long the bakeries would be baking fresh bread, the cafés would be opening, and all the little comforts and joys of Paris could be mine again. I was lost and in the dark, but I was also lost in the dark in Paris, and that held a kind of magic that I might never experience again.

I got off my bike, pulled it up to the sidewalk, kicked out the stand, and rested it there. I arched my back and looked up at the sky. It was a cloudy night. I took a deep breath and then another. Not since I was a kid had I been lost like this, and certainly not in such an uncomfortable position. The trick is to keep your composure, to go slowly and carefully. I had allowed myself to be caught up in the excitement and had made mistakes. I needed to gather myself, then try again. I had my Vélib. And somewhere not too far was the Seine. I would find my way. It might take longer than I thought. But I would find my way.

I tried my phone one last time and when the little apple lit up I held my breath. It was working. Even so, I knew I only had a few moments of battery left. This might be the last time my phone would turn on, so I had to take advantage of it.

The map opened. My location appeared, and I discovered I was at Place de Nations. Somehow, instead of going southwest, I had managed to go south-by-southeast. If I had continued in the direction I had been going I would never even have reached the Seine, could have biked my way out of Paris.

But now I also knew where to go. I turned my phone off,

got back on my bike, and took the first exit out of the roundabout toward Rue du Faubourg Saint-Antoine. It was a
beautiful street, lined with trees that were just beginning to
bud with early spring leaves. I rode the street for what
seemed like a very long time. Then I saw the road was turning, and around the turn there it was, a giant glowing green
tower: Place de la Bastille.

I probably should have stopped. The Bastille is one of
those places you're supposed to visit when you're in Paris,
this memento of the French Revolution that lives on as a
symbol of freedom but also of violence and foolishness.

I didn't pause, though, and I didn't even think about
the Bastille and what it meant. It was too late. I was ready
to be home, to be warm, and in places I recognized. I knew
it was close to 2:30 now and so I rode around the roundabout and took the wrong turn, but by now I was close
enough that I couldn't mess up too badly, and then there
was a sign for Châtelet and I knew Châtelet and so I
turned.

The pedals turned easily and Paris rose up around me
and I was flying through the streets and I was free. I saw
strings of lights down a side street and on a whim I turned
my bike down the street, the wheels coasting on my momentum. The asphalt was wet and reflective of the lights and the
sky above and there were a few people still out or else
leaving the doors finally closing for the night and there was
the sound of laughter and the smell of seafood. I kept
pedaling into the heart of Paris.

I came upon a great building. In Paris, there are many
great buildings, and some of them you pass by without a
second thought not even realizing their importance, but this
building had steepled towers and huge square in front of it
was impossible to dismiss. Hôtel de Ville it said somewhere,

and I thought, *This is a hotel? Or once was a hotel? It's far too big and ornate to be a hotel. Who could afford it?*[1]

But then my Vélib had taken me past it and suddenly I was on the Seine.

"Thank you. Thank you, Paris. Thank you, God. I've made it." I had crossed the Seine then and I was on Île de la Cité and then there was Notre Dame. I rode into the square and over the marker that symbolizes the center of France, and I marvelled because somehow I had brought myself there and Notre Dame looked as if it was on fire, all orange and yellow and green. It was almost three in the morning now and I had to get home, but this moment was magic and I didn't want it to end.

"Goodbye, Notre Dame," I said because you can't hold on to anything forever.

"Goodbye, Notre Dame," because every moment is a vapor disappearing into wind and even if you saw Notre Dame again it would never be like this.

"Goodbye, river Seine," because I was riding past it now and every drop of its water was heading for the sea, but even so the sea would never be full.

"Goodbye, Shakespeare and Co.," because you can always have books, but how do you match the experience of a book bought in Paris?

"Goodbye, Pont des Arts," because you can never have enough love or art, but I was turning now away from it all and heading down Rue de Seine and I was going fast, my heart beating from the joy of it all.

"Goodbye, Paris," because I was putting my Vélib back in the stand not far from my flat and my legs felt empty as if they were filled not with blood and muscle but with vapor and because I had only discovered Paris in this moment and it was already fleeing me because what you learn as a writer is that you can capture anything in words except no one will remember them forever and soon even the words are lost to time's ceaseless march. Every moment is dying. Every moment is being remade anew.

I woke as the bus was pulling into a small, dismal airport. We checked in for our budget flight, ate cheap food that Talia turned her nose up to.

Then we were on a plane with uncomfortable seats. Our plane took off. I held Talia's hand and she held mine. Food and drinks were extra so there was nothing to do but sit there, holding hands.

We landed after dark in Pisa. There was more adventure after that. A few family fights. More wine. More getting lost but in Florence and Rome, not Paris.

Grandma did not end up getting married in Florence. "Too much trouble," she told me. She's still engaged, but she will probably stay that way. She's still ten years older than her fiancé, but she's thirty years more fun.

Goodbye, France.

Goodbye, Paris.

We had a nice time, and sometimes not so nice a time, but there is no other city like you.

Goodbye. Au revoir. I'll see you again soon.

Thank you for reading *Crowdsourcing Paris*. I hope you enjoyed it. If you did, please leave a review. Your reviews help fuel the success of this series.

By the way, you can get a free Paris walking guide, just for subscribing at crowdsourcingadventure.com. See you there.

NOTES

1. Paris

1. Thanks to William Warren for first explaining this to me.

2. Caves

1. Talia disputes this.

3. Directions

1. Talia contests this.
2. Let's be honest: Not a day without a map, because who carries maps anymore? It was a day without *Google* Maps! How I would have survived in that country without that Silicon Valley company, I have no idea (don't you think they should really be sponsoring this book, I've said their names so many times?)

5. Painting

1. http://www.newyorker.com/magazine/1950/05/13/how-do-you-like-it-now-gentlemen

6. French Onion Soup

1. Find a full list of what every state in the U.S. is known for here: https://www.foodnetwork.com/restaurants/packages/best-food-in-america/photos/most-iconic-food-united-states

7. Street Performer

1. Like so many, watching Notre Dame burn down on the news was a tragic experience. Anyone who argues that the money donated to its

rebuilding effort is a waste, that the money would be better spent on more pressing needs, doesn't understand humanity's need for awe, that awe is a resource as dear as food, and that it should be cultivated and protected.

8. Chef

1. From "Chariot" by Page France

Epilogue: Home

1. It took me months to learn that the Hôtel de Ville is the city hall of Paris and not, in fact, a hotel to accommodate travellers. So now you know, if you happen to stumble on it in the middle of the night.

ACKNOWLEDGMENTS

Every book is crowdsourced. Every book is the product of many hands. There are many whom, without their help, this book would not have happened.

First, thanks to Talia, without whom none of this would have been possible. A wise man once told me that he never accomplished any of his dreams until he married his wife. That has been true of my life as well. Thank you for being my adventure partner, Talia. I love you.

Thanks also to Seth, who has incited many of my adventures, and who continues to challenge me to reach my potential today, and also to Max Dubinsky, who was the first non-family member to see the potential of this project and how to make it good.

Special thanks to Jeff Goins for asking me a hundred times over the last five years, "How's that Paris book coming," to Tim Grahl for giving me the structure I needed to make it happen, and to Jeff Shinabarger and my Layers group for keeping up the pressure. Without all of your help I'd still be working on this book.

Thanks also to Shawn Coyne for identifying the soul of

this story, to Alice Sudlow, my editor, who helped me make this book "work" and put up with at least *some* of my grammar decisions, and to Joy Reed, my agent, who believed in this book even when a lot of people didn't.

Thanks to my contributors, especially to Tim Abare, Michael Price, Ross Boone, Beau Henderson, Nichole Rhodes, Audrey Chin, and Jane Babich. Without you, we would never have been able to make this journey happen. Also thanks to Michael Bunting, Eric Hanson, Bill Bush, Teri Frana, Christine Hein, Arwen Eleanor Whiting, Carson Gleberman, Alexandros Stamatiou, Miles Tiegs, Mirel Bodner Abeles, Katie Hamer, Kevin Weiler, Pamela, Arlen Miller, Fiona Raye Clarke, Taisa Skovorodko, Shireen Lim, Guillaumeh, Patience Grace, Debbie Steg, Martyn Chamberlin, Scott Taylor, Shane Tilston, Rob Skidmore, Gretchen Hunter, Rebecca Pavlick, Mark Gottlieb, Emily Mance, Kacie Price, Kristin Rene, Terrence Cleary, Wayne Bailey, Carlos Cooper, Katina Vaselopulos, Zak Erving, Daniel Stinson, Tore Johnson, Felicia Stanford, Dawn Oshima, Max Andrew Dubinsky, Philip Dunlop, Janelle White, Iris Bianchin, Sharon Olson, Melissa Mayer, Jesse Stanford, Abby Kitchin, Etienne, Stephanie Pridgen, Steven Garriott, Suzanne G, Kathy, Leanne Smith, Stacey Covell, B. Rasine, Catherine Morrell, Jessica Martensen, Jess Eischens, Annie Carter, Mark Foley, Eliza Jane Kennelly, Lisa Nelson, Terrie Coleman, Michael Mardel, Nicky Cahill, Sarah Freeman, Rochelle Comeaux, Laure Reminick, L. V., Abigail Rogers, Beca Lewis, Nicole Gent, Parker, Victoria M. Johnson, Michelle Cecilia De Bruyn, and Cat Thibault.

Thanks to my beta readers, especially Margherita Crystal Lotus, Jay Warner, Jeff Elkins, Jessica Bennet, and Karen Anderson.

Finally, thank you to the readers of The Write Practice,

who made it possible for me to be a writer. I'm honored to have your trust and attention. Thanks for coming to Paris with me.

Books are a community effort, a crowdsourced effort, and I'm so grateful for my community. I don't take it for granted. I'm looking forward to our next adventure.

CPSIA information can be obtained
at www.ICGtesting.com
Printed in the USA
FFHW020934121019
55527443-61329FF